NATURE MYSTICI...

(1913)

SYMBOLIC REPRESENTATION OF THE BIRTH OF
THE PHILOSOPHER'S STONE
Triomphe Hermetique (1689)

**Contents: Nature and the Absolute; Mystic Intuition and
Reason; Man and Nature; Mystic Receptivity; Animism,
Ancient and Modern; Will and Consciousness in Nature;
Mythology; Poetry and Nature Mysticism; Rivers of Life
and Death; Earth, Air, Fire, and Water; Light and Darkness;
Seasons, Vegetations, and Animals, plus much more.**

J. Edward Mercer

ISBN 1-56459-583-8

Kessinger Publishing Company
Montana, U.S.A.

PREFACE

THE aims of this study of Nature Mysticism, and the methods adopted for attaining them, are sufficiently described in the introductory chapter. It may be said, by way of special preface, that the nature mystic here portrayed is essentially a " modern." He is assumed to have accepted the fundamentals of the hypothesis of evolution. Accordingly, his sympathy with the past is profound : so also is his sense of the reality and continuity of human development, physical, psychic, and mystical. Moreover, he tries to be abreast of the latest critical and scientific conclusions. Imperfections manifold will be discovered in the pages that follow ; but the author asks that a percentage of them may be attributed to the difficulties of writing in Tasmania and publishing at the antipodes.

J. E. M.

BISHOP'S COURT, HOBART,
March, 1912.

CONTENTS

CHAPTER   PAGE

    I.   INTRODUCTORY   1

   II.   NATURE, AND THE ABSOLUTE   7

  III.   MYSTIC INTUITION AND REASON   15

  IV.   MAN AND NATURE   23

   V.   MYSTIC RECEPTIVITY   30

  VI.   DEVELOPMENT AND DISCIPLINE OF INTUITION   38

 VII.   NATURE NOT SYMBOLIC   45

VIII.   THE CHARGE OF ANTHROPOMORPHISM   54

  IX.   THE IMMANENT IDEA   65

   X.   ANIMISM, ANCIENT AND MODERN   71

  XI.   WILL AND CONSCIOUSNESS IN NATURE   79

 XII.   MYTHOLOGY   90

XIII.   POETRY AND NATURE MYSTICISM   97

 XIV.   THE BEAUTIFUL AND THE UGLY   106

  XV.   NATURE MYSTICISM AND THE RACE   117

 XVI.   THALES   123

XVII.   THE WATERS UNDER THE EARTH   129

XVIII.   SPRINGS AND WELLS   138

 XIX.   BROOKS AND STREAMS   145

Nature Mysticism

CHAPTER		PAGE
XX.	Rivers and Life	151
XXI.	Rivers and Death	158
XXII.	The Ocean	165
XXIII.	Waves	172
XXIV.	Still Waters	179
XXV.	Anaximenes and the Air	187
XXVI.	Winds and Clouds	192
XXVII.	Heracleitus and the Cosmic Fire	203
XXVIII.	Fire and the Sun	211
XXIX.	Light and Darkness	222
XXX.	The Expanse of Heaven—Colour	228
XXXI.	The Moon—A Special Problem	235
XXXII.	Earth, Mountains, and Plains	242
XXXIII.	Seasons, Vegetation, Animals	248
XXXIV.	Pragmatic	257

NATURE MYSTICISM

CHAPTER I

INTRODUCTORY

A WAVE of Mysticism is passing over the civilised nations. It is welcomed by many : by more it is mistrusted. Even the minds to which it would naturally appeal are often restrained from sympathy by fears of vague speculative driftings and of transcendental emotionalism. Nor can it be doubted that such an attitude of aloofness is at once reasonable and inevitable. For a systematic exaltation of formless ecstasies, at the expense of sense and intellect, has a tendency to become an infirmity if it does not always betoken loss of mental balance. In order, therefore, to disarm natural prejudice, let an opening chapter be devoted to general exposition of aims and principles.

The subject is Nature Mysticism. The phenomena of "nature" are to be studied in their mystical aspects. The wide term Mysticism is used because, in spite of many misleading associations, it is hard to replace. "Love of nature" is

B

Nature Mysticism

too general : " cosmic emotion " is too specialised.
But let it at once be understood that the Mysticism
here contemplated is neither of the popular nor of
the esoteric sort. In other words, it is not loosely
synonymous with the magical or supernatural ;
nor is it a name for peculiar forms of ecstatic experience which claim to break away from the
spheres of the senses and the intellect. It will
simply be taken to cover the causes and the effects
involved in that wide range of intuitions and
emotions which nature stimulates without definite
appeal to conscious reasoning processes. Mystic
intuition and mystic emotion will thus be regarded,
not as antagonistic to sense impression, but as dependent on it—not as scornful of reason, but merely
as more basic and primitive.

Science describes nature, but it cannot *feel*
nature ; still less can it account for that sense of
kinship with nature which is so characteristic of
many of the foremost thinkers of the day. For
life is more and more declaring itself to be something fuller than a blind play of physical forces,
however complex and sublimated their interactions.
It reveals a ceaseless striving—an *élan vital* (as
Bergson calls it) to expand and enrich the forms
of experience—a reaching forward to fuller beauty
and more perfect order.

A certain amount of metaphysical discussion
will be necessary ; but it will be reduced to the
minimum compatible with coherency. Fortunately, Nature Mysticism can be at home with

2

Introductory

diverse world-views. There is, however, one exception—the world-view which is based on the concept of an Unconditioned Absolute. This will be unhesitatingly rejected as subversive of any genuine "communion" with nature. So also Symbolism will be repudiated on the ground that it furnishes a quite inadequate account of the relation of natural phenomena to the human mind. The only metaphysical theory adopted, as a generalised working basis, is that known as Ideal-Realism. It assumes three spheres of existence—that which in a peculiar sense is *within* the individual mind : that which in a peculiar sense is *without* (external to) the individual mind : and that in which these two are fused or come into living contact. It will be maintained, as a thesis fundamental to Nature Mysticism, that the world of external objects must be essentially of the same essence as the perceiving minds. The bearing of these condensed statements will become plain as the phenomena of nature are passed in review. Of formal theology there will be none.

The more certain conclusions of modern science, including the broader generalisations of the hypothesis of evolution, will be assumed. Lowell, in one of his sonnets, says :

> " I grieve not that ripe knowledge takes away
>   The charm that nature to my childhood wore
>   For, with that insight cometh, day by day,
>   A greater bliss than wonder was before :

3

Nature Mysticism

The real doth not clip the poet's wings ;
  To win the secret of a weed's plain heart
Reveals some clue to spiritual things,
  And stumbling guess becomes firm-rooted art."

Admirable—as far as it goes ! But the modern nature-mystic cannot rest content with the last line. The aim of nature-insight is not art, however firm-rooted ; for art is, so to speak, a secondary product, a reflection. The goal of the nature-mystic is actual living communion with the Real, in and through its sensuous manifestations.

Nature Mysticism, as thus conceived, does not seek to glorify itself above other modes of experience and psychic activity. The partisanship of the theological or of the transcendental type is here condemned. Nor will there be an appeal to any ecstatic faculty which can only be the vaunted appanage of the few. The appeal will lie to faculties which are shared in some degree by all normal human beings, though they are too often neglected, if not disparaged. Rightly developed, the capacity for entering into communion with nature is not only a source of the purest pleasure, but a subtle and powerful agent in aiding men to realise some of the noblest potentialities of their being.

When treating of specific natural phenomena, the exposition demands proof and illustration. In certain chapters, therefore, quotations from the prose and poetry of those ancients and moderns who, avowedly or unavowedly, rank as nature-

4

Introductory

mystics, are freely introduced. These extracts
form an integral part of the study, because they
afford direct evidence of the reality, and of the
continuity, of the mystical faculty as above
defined.

The usual method of procedure will be to trace
the influence of certain selected natural phenomena
on the human mind, first in the animistic stage,
then in the mythological stage, and lastly in the
present, with a view to showing that there has
been a genuine and living development of deep-
seated nature intuitions. But this method will
not be too strictly followed. Special subjects
will meet with special treatment, and needless
repetition will be carefully avoided. The various
chapters, as far as may be, will not only present
new themes, but will approach the subject at
different angles.

It is obvious that severe limitations must be
imposed in the selection from so vast a mass of
material. Accordingly, the phenomena of Water,
Air, and Fire have received the fullest attention—
the first of the triad getting the lion's share; but
other marked features of the physical universe
have not been altogether passed by. The realm
of organic life—vegetable and animal—does not
properly fall within the limits of this study. For
where organised life reveals itself, men find it less
difficult to realise their kinship with existences
other than human. The curious, and still obscure,
history of totemism supplies abundant evidence

Nature Mysticism

on this point; and not less so that modern sympathy with all living things, which is largely based on what may be termed the new totemism of the Darwinian theory. But while attention will thus be focussed on the sphere of the inorganic, seemingly so remote from human modes of experience, some attempt will nevertheless be made to suggest the inner harmonies which link together all modes of existence. A further limitation to be noted is that "nature" will be taken to cover only such natural objects as remain in what is generally called their "natural" condition—that is, which are independent of, and unaffected by, human activities.

Let Goethe, in his Faust hymn, tell what is the heart and essence of Nature Mysticism as here to be expounded and defended.

> "Rears not the heaven its arch above?
>   Doth not the firm-set earth beneath us lie?
> And with the tender gaze of love
>   Climb not the everlasting stars on high?
>   Do I not gaze upon thee, eye to eye?
> And all the world of sight and sense and sound,
>   Bears it not in upon thy heart and brain,
> And mystically weave around
>   Thy being influences that never wane?"

6

CHAPTER II

NATURE, AND THE ABSOLUTE

As just stated, metaphysics and theology are to be avoided. But since Mysticism is generally associated with belief in an Unconditioned Absolute, and since such an Absolute is fatal to the claims of any genuine Nature Mysticism, a preliminary flying incursion into the perilous regions must be ventured.

Mysticism in its larger sense is admittedly difficult to define. It connotes a vast group of special experiences and speculations which deal with material supposed to be beyond the reach of sense and reason. It carries us back to the strangely illusive "mysteries" of the Greeks, but is more definitely used in connection with the most characteristic subtleties of the wizard East, and with certain developments of the Platonic philosophy. Extended exposition is not required. Suffice it to state what may fairly be regarded as the three fundamental principles, or doctrines, on which mystics of the orthodox schools generally depend. These principles will be subjected to a free but friendly criticism : considerable modifications will be suggested, and the way thus prepared

7

Nature Mysticism

for the study of Nature Mysticism properly so-called.

The three principles alluded to are the following. First, the true mystic is one possessed by a desire to have communion with the ultimately Real. Second, the ultimately Real is to be regarded as a supersensuous, super-rational, and unconditional Absolute—the mystic One. Third, the direct communion for which the mystic yearns—the *unio mystica*—cannot be attained save by passive contemplation, resulting in vision, insight, or ecstasy.

With a view to giving a definite and concrete turn to the critical examination of these three fundamentals, let us take a passage from a recently published booklet. The author tells how that on a certain sunny afternoon he flung himself down on the bank of a brimming mill-stream. The weir was smoothly flowing: the mill-wheel still. He meditates on the scene and concludes thus: " Perhaps we are never so receptive as when with folded hands we say simply, ' This is a great mystery.' I watched and wondered until Jem called, and I had to leave the rippling weir and the water's side, and the wheel with its untold secret."

There are certain forms, or modes, of experience here presented which are at least mystical in their tendency—the sense of a deeper reality than that which can be grasped by conscious reason—a desire to penetrate a secret that will not yield

8

Nature, and the Absolute

itself to articulate thought and which nevertheless leaves a definite impress on the mind. There
is also a recognition of the passive attitude which
the ordinary mystic doctrine avers to be essential
to vision. Will these features warrant our regarding the experiences as genuinely mystical?

The answer to this question brings into bold
relief a vital difference between orthodox mystics
and those here called nature-mystics, and raises
the issue on which the very existence of a valid
Nature Mysticism must depend. The stricter
schools would unhesitatingly refuse to accord to
such experiences the right to rank with those
which result in true insight. Why? Because
they obviously rest on sense impressions. An
English mystic, for example, states in a recent
article that Mysticism is always and necessarily
extra-phenomenal, and that the man who tries
to elucidate the visible by means of the invisible
is no true mystic; still less, of course, the man
who tries to elucidate the invisible by means of
the visible. The true mystic, he says, fixes his
eyes on eternity and the infinite; he loses himself
when he becomes entangled in the things of time,
that is, in the phenomenal. Still more explicit is
the statement of a famous modern Yogi. " This
world is a delusive charm of the great magician
called Mâya. . . . Mâya has imagined infinite
illusions called the different things in the universe.
. . . The minds which have not attained to the
Highest, and are a prey to natural beauties in

Nature Mysticism

the stage of Mâya, will continually have to turn into various forms, from one to another, because nothing in the stage of Mâya is stable." Nor would the Christian mystics allow of any intermediaries between the soul and God; they most of them held that the soul must rise above the things of sense, mount into another sphere, and be " alone with the Alone."

What, then, is the concept of the ultimately Real which these stricter mystics have evolved and are prepared to defend? It is that of pure and unconditioned Being—the One—the Absolute. By a ruthless process of abstraction they have abjured the world of sense to vow allegiance to a mode of being of which nothing can be said without denying it. For even to allow a shadow of finiteness in the Absolute is to negate it; to define it is to annihilate it! It swallows up all conditions and relations without becoming any more knowable; it embraces everything and remains a pure negation. It lies totally and eternally beyond the reach of man's faculties and yet demands his perfect and unreasoning surrender. A concept, this, born of the brains of logical Don Quixotes.

And it is for such a monstrous abstraction we are asked to give up the full rich world of sense, with all it means to us. It is surely not an intellectual weakness to say: " Tell us what you will of existence above and beyond that which is known to us; but do not deny some measure of ultimate Reality to that which falls within our

Nature, and the Absolute

ken. Leave us not alone with the Absolute of the orthodox mystic, or we perish of inanity! Clearly the *élan vital*—the will to live—gives us a more hopeful starting-point in our search for the Real. Clearly the inexhaustible variety of the universe of sense need not be dubbed an illusion to save the consistency of a logic which has not yet succeeded in grasping its own first principles. No, the rippling weir and the mill-wheel were real in their own degree, and the intuitions and emotions they prompted were the outcome of a contact between the inner and the outer—a *unio mystica*—a communion between the soul of a man and the soul in the things he saw.

"But" (says the orthodox mystic) "there is a special form of craving—the craving for the Infinite. Man cannot find rest save in communion with a supreme Reality free from all imperfections and limitations; and such a Reality can be found in nothing less than the Unconditioned Absolute." Now we may grant the existence and even the legitimacy of the craving thus emphatically asserted while questioning the form which it is made to assume. The man gazing at the mill-wheel longed to know its secret. Suppose he had succeeded! We think of Tennyson's "little flower in the crannied wall." We think of Blake's lines:

> " To see the world in a grain of sand,
> And a heaven in a wild flower,
> Hold infinity in the palm of your hand,
> And eternity in an hour."

11

Nature Mysticism

Is it really necessary to forsake the finite to reach the infinite—whatever that term may be taken to mean? Do we not often better realise the infinity of the sky by looking at it through the twigs of a tree?

For the craving itself, in its old mystic form, we can have nothing but sympathy. Some of its expressions are wonderfully touching, but their pathos must not blind us to the maimed character of the world-view on which they rest. Grant that the sphere of sense is limited and therefore imperfect, let it at any rate be valid up to the limit it does actually attain. The rippling weir and the mill-wheel did produce some sort of effect upon the beholder, and therefore must have been to that extent real. What do we gain by flinging away the chance to learn, even though the gain be small? And if, as the nature-mystic claims, the gain be great, the folly is proportionately intensified.

Coleridge is quoted as an exponent of the feeling of the stricter mystics.

> " It were a vain endeavour,
>   Though I should gaze for ever
> On the green light that lingers in the West ;
> I may not hope from outward forms to win
> The passion and the life whose fountains are within."

This, however, is too gentle and hesitating, too tinged with love of nature, to convey the fierce conviction of the consistent devotee of the Absolute, of the defecated transparency of pure Being.

Nature, and the Absolute

If, as is urged by Récéjac, we find among some of the stricter mystics a very deep and naïve feeling for nature, such feeling can only be a sign of inconsistency, a yielding to the solicitations of the lower nature. Granted their premisses, the world of sense can teach nothing. It is well to face this issue squarely—let the mystic choose, either the Absolute and Mâya, or a Ground of existence which can allow value to nature, and which therefore admits of limitations. Or, if there is to be a compromise, let it be on the lines laid down by Spinoza and Schelling. That is to say, let the name God be reserved for the phenomenal aspect of the Absolute. But the nature-mystic will be wise if he discards compromise, and once for all repudiates the Unconditioned Absolute. His reason can then chime in with his intuitions and his deepest emotions. He loses nothing ; he gains intellectual peace and natural joy.

The never-ceasing influence of the genuine Real is bound to declare itself sooner or later. Buddhism itself is yielding, as witness this striking pronouncement of the Buddhist Lord Abbot, Soyen Shaku. " Buddhism does not, though sometimes understood by Western people to do so, advocate the doctrine of emptiness or annihilation. It most assuredly recognises the multitudinousness and reality of phenomena. This world as it is, is real, not void. This life, as we live it, is true, and not a dream. We Buddhists believe that all these particular things surround-

13

Nature Mysticism

ing us come from one Ultimate Source, all-knowing and all-loving. The world is the manifestation of this Reason, or Spirit, or Life, whatever you may designate it. However diverse, therefore, things are, they all partake of the nature of the Ultimate Being. Not only sentient beings, but non-sentient, reflect the glory of the Original Reason."

Assuredly a comforting passage to set over against that of the Yogi quoted above! But is not the good Abbot a little hard on the Westerners? For the full truth is that while the Yogi represents the old Absolutism, the Abbot is feeling his way to a wider and more human world-view. Buddhism has evidently better days in store. Let our views of ultimate Reality be what they may, the nature-mystic's position demands not only that man may hold communion with nature, but that, in and through such communion, he is in living touch with the Ground of Existence.

CHAPTER III

MYSTIC INTUITION AND REASON

So much for the nature-mystic's relation to the
concept of the Absolute. It would be interesting
to discuss, from the same point of view, his relations to the rival doctrines of the monists, dualists,
and pluralists. But to follow up these trails with
any thoroughness would lead us too far into the
thickets and quagmires of metaphysics. Fortunately the issues are not nearly so vital as in the
case of the Absolute; and they may thus be
passed by without serious risk of invalidating
subsequent conclusions. It may be worth our
while, however, to note that many modern mystics
are not monists, and that the supposed inseparable
connection between Mysticism and Monism is being
thrown overboard. Even the older mystics, when
wrestling with the problem of evil, were dualists
in their own despite. Of the moderns, so representative a thinker as Lotze suggested that
Reality may run up, not into one solitary peak,
but into a mountain chain. Höffding contends
that we have not yet gained the right to career
rough-shod over the antinomies of existence.
James, a typical modern mystic, was an avowed

15

Nature Mysticism

pluralist. Bergson emphasises the category of Becoming, and, if to be classed at all, is a dualist. Thus the nature-mystic is happy in the freedom to choose his own philosophy, so long as he avoids the toils of the Absolute. For, as James remarks, " oneness and manyness are absolutely co-ordinate. Neither is primordial or more excellent than the other."

It remains, then, to subject to criticism the third principle of Mysticism, that of intuitional insight as a mode of knowing independent of the reasoning faculties, at any rate in their conscious exercise. Its root idea is that of directness and immediacy ; the word itself prepares us for some power of apprehending at a glance—a power which dispenses with all process and gains its end by a flash. A higher stage is known as vision ; the highest is known as ecstasy. Intuition has its own place in general psychology, and has acquired peculiar significance in the domains of æsthetics, ethics, and theology ; and the same root idea is preserved throughout—that of immediacy of insight. The characteristic of passivity on which certain mystics would insist is subsidiary—even if it is to be allowed at all. Its claims will be noted later.

Now Nature Mysticism is based on sense perception, and this in itself is a form of intuition. It is immediate, for the " matter " of sensation presents itself directly to the consciousness affected ; it simply asserts itself. It is indepen-

16

Mystic Intuition and Reason

dent of the conscious exercise of the reasoning powers. It does not even permit of the distinction between subject and object; it comes into the mind as " a given." When conscious thought grips this " given," it can put it into all manner of relations with other " givens." It may even to some extent control the course of subsequent sensations by the exercise of attention and in accordance with a conscious purpose. But thought cannot create a sensation. The sensation is thus at the base of all mental life. It furnishes material for the distinction between subject and object—between the outer and the inner. The conscious processes, thus primed, rise through the various stages of contemplation, reflection, abstraction, conception, and reasoning.

The study of sense perception is thus seen to be a study of primary mystical intuition. But the similarity, or essential bond, between the two may be worked at a deeper level. When an external object stimulates a sensation, it produces a variety of changes in the mind of the percipient. Most of these may remain in the depths of subconscious mental life, but they are none the less real as effectual agents of change. Now what is here implied ? The external object has somehow or other got " inside " the percipient mind—has penetrated to it, and modified it. In other words, a form of mystical communion has been established. The object has penetrated into the mind, and the mind has come into living touch with the

Nature Mysticism

Real external to itself. The object and the subject are to this extent fused in a mystic union. How could the fusion take place unless the two were linked in some fundamental harmony of being? Other and higher modes of mystical union may be experienced; but sense perception contains them all in germ. How vain, then, the absolutist's attempt to sever himself from the sphere of sense!

Intuition, we have seen, must be deemed to be independent of conscious reasoning processes. But this is not to say that it is independent of reason, either objectively or subjectively. Not objectively, for if the world is a cosmos, it must be rationally constituted. Not subjectively, for man's reasoning faculties may influence many of his mental activities without rising to the level of reflective ratiocination. And thus man's communion with the cosmos, of which he is himself a part, will be grounded in the reason which permeates the whole.

If we go on to ask what is the relation between intuition and conscious reflective processes, the answer would seem to be somewhat of this kind. Intuition, in its wide sense, furnishes material; reason works it up. Intuition moves about in worlds not systematised; reason reduces them to order. Reflective thought dealing with the phenomena presented to it by sensation has three tasks before it—to find out the nature of the objects, to trace their causes, and to trace their

18

Mystic Intuition and Reason

effects. And whereas each intuitional experience stands alone and isolated in its immediacy, reason groups these single experiences together, investigates their conditions, and makes them subserve definite conscious purposes.

But if mystics have too often made the mistake of underrating the powers and functions of reflective reason, the champions of logic have also been guilty of the counter-mistake of disparaging intuition, more especially that called mystical. That is to say, the *form* of thought is declared to be superior to the *matter* of thought—a truly remarkable contention! What is reason if it has no material to work up? And whence comes the material but from sensation and intuition? Moreover, even when the material is furnished to the reasoning processes, the conclusions arrived at have to be brought continuously and relentlessly to the bar, not only of physical fact, but also to that of intuition and sentiment, if serious errors are to be avoided. Systematising and speculative zeal have a tendency to run ahead of their data.

Bergson has done much to restore to intuition the rights which were being filched or wrenched from it. He has shown (may it be said conclusively?) that systematised thought is quite unequal to grappling with the processes which constitute actual living. Before him, Schopenhauer had poured well-deserved contempt on the idea that the brain, an organ which can only work

19

for a few hours at a stretch, and is dependent
on all the accidents of the physical condition of
the body, should be considered equal to solving
the problems of existence. "Certainly" (writes
Schwegler) "the highest truths of reason, the
eternal, the divine, are not to be proved by means
of demonstration." But this is no less true of the
simplest manifestations of reality. Knowledge is
compelled to move on the surface when it aims
at scientific method and demonstrated results.
Intuitive knowledge can often penetrate deeper,
get nearer to the heart of things and divine
their deeper relations. When intuitions can be
gripped by conscious reasoning processes, man
gains much of the knowledge which is power.
But the scope of knowledge in the fullest sense
is indefinitely greater than that of science and
philosophy.˙

Nor is it hard to see why the sphere of reflective
thought is thus comparatively limited. For
modern speculations, and even the straitest psychology, have familiarised us with the idea of a
larger self that is beyond the reach of conscious
analysis. Obscure workings of the mind—emotions, moods, immediate perceptions, premonitions, and the rest—have a potent part to play
in the actual living of a life. Consider in this connection such a passage as the following, taken
from Jefferies' "Story of My Heart." It means
something, though it is not scientific.

"Three things only have been discovered of that

20

Mystic Intuition and Reason

which concerns the inner consciousness since before
written history began. Three things only in twelve
thousand written, or sculptured years, and in the
dumb, dim time before them. Three ideas the
cavemen wrested from the unknown, the night
which is round us still in daylight—*the existence
of the soul, immortality, the deity.* These things
. . . do not suffice me. I desire to advance
farther, and to wrest a fourth, and even still more
than a fourth, from the darkness of thought. I
want more ideas of soul-life. . . . My naked
mind confronts the unknown. I see as clearly as
the noonday that this is not all ; I see other and
higher conditions than existence ; I see not only
the existence of the soul, but, in addition, I
realise a soul-life illimitable. . . . I strive to give
utterance to a Fourth Idea. The very idea that
there is another idea is something gained. The
three gained by the cavemen are but stepping-
stones, first links of an endless chain."

Of course, we are here reminded of Wordsworth's " obstinate questionings of sense and outward things " ; of his " misgivings of a creature
moving about in worlds not realised." Intuition
is feeling its way outwards beyond the sphere of
the known, and emotion is working in harmony
with it, the reason still fails to grip. Morris'
description of a like sense of unrealised possibilities applies, in varying degrees, to men of all
sorts and conditions, though the poets of whom
he speaks are the most favoured.

21

Nature Mysticism

" Blind thoughts which occupy the brain,
　Dumb melodies which fill the ear,
Dim perturbations, precious pain,
　A gleam of hope, a chill of fear—
These seize the poet's soul, and mould
The ore of fancy into gold."

Language is thus employed to proclaim its own inadequacy. And who can fail to see that between the rich complexity of the workings of the whole mind and the means by which we would fain render them articulate, there yawns a gap which no effort can bridge over ? Even the poet fails—much more the scientist ! To refuse to take cognisance of the fresh spontaneity of feeling and intuition is to rob life of its higher joys and its deeper meanings.

CHAPTER IV

MAN AND NATURE

MANY thinkers of the present day pride themselves upon the growth of what they call the naturalistic spirit. What do they mean by this ? They mean that the older ways of interpreting nature, animistic or supernatural, are being supplanted by explanations founded on knowledge of physical facts and " natural " laws. And, up to a point, there are but few natural mystics who will not concur in their feelings of satisfaction that ignorance and superstition are disappearing in rough proportion as exact knowledge advances. At any rate, in this study, the more solid conclusions of science will be freely and gladly accepted. The very idea of a conflict between Science and Natural Mysticism is to be mercilessly scouted.

But this concurrence must be conditional. Tait, for example, was scornful of any form of animism. He wrote thus : " The Pygmalions of modern days do not require to beseech Aphrodité to animate the world for them. Like the savage with his Totem, they have themselves already attributed life to it. ' It comes,' as Helmholtz says, ' to the same thing as Schopenhauer's metaphysics. The stars are to love and hate one another, feel pleasure and displeasure, and to try to move in a way corresponding to these feelings.' The latest phase of this peculiar non-science tells us that all matter is ALIVE; or at least that it contains the 'promise and potency' (whatever these may be) 'of all terrestrial life.' All this probably originated in the very simple manner already hinted at; viz., in the confusion of terms constructed for application to thinking beings only, with others applicable only to brute matter, and a blind following of this confusion to its necessarily preposterous consequences. So much for the attempts to introduce into science an element altogether incompatible with the fundamental conditions of its existence."

This is vigorous! But how does the matter now stand? Since Tait wrote his invective, many physicists of at least equal rank with himself, and with some undreamt-of discoveries to the good, have subscribed to the views which he so trenchantly condemns. As for the metaphysicians, there are but few of the first flight who do not conceive of consciousness as the ultimate form of existence. Again, the reference to the Pygmalion myth implies the view that mythology was a mere empty product of untutored fancy and imaginative subjectivism. Here also he is out of harmony with the spirit now pervading the science of religion and the comparative study of early modes of belief. It will be well to devote some chapters to

Man and Nature

a survey of the problems thus suggested, and to preface them by an enquiry, on general lines, into man's relation to nature.

We shall best come to grips with the real issue by fastening on Tait's " brute matter." For the words contain a whole philosophy. On the one hand, matter, inert, lifeless : on the other hand, spirit, living, supersensuous : between the two, and linking the two, man, a spirit in a body. Along with this there generally goes a dogma of special creations, though it may perhaps be held that such a dogma is not essential to the distinction between the two realms thus sharply sundered. It is at once obvious that, starting from such premisses, Tait's invective is largely justified. For if matter is inert, brute, dead—it certainly seems preposterous to speak of its having within it the potency of life—using " life " as a synonym for living organisms, including man. The nature-mystic is overwhelmed with Homeric laughter.

But the whole trend of scientific investigation and speculation is increasingly away from this crude and violent dualism. The relation of soul to body is still a burning question, but does not at all preclude a belief that matter is one mode of the manifestation of spirit. Indeed, it is hard to understand how upholders of the disappearing doctrine would ever bring themselves to maintain, even on their own premisses, that any creation of the Supreme Spirit could be " brute "—that is, inert and irrational ! Regarded from the new

25

Nature Mysticism

view-point, all is what may, for present purposes, be called spiritual. And when man appeared upon the globe, he was not something introduced from without, different from and alien to the world of matter, but merely the outcome of a more intense activity of the same forces as were at work from the first and in the whole—in brief, a higher manifestation of the life which is the ultimate Ground of all modes of existence. There are not two different realms, that of brute matter and living spirit ; but various planes, or grades, of life and consciousness. Leibniz had the beautiful and profound idea that life has three modes on earth—it sleeps in plants, it dreams in animals, and it wakes in man. Modern thought is expanding, universalising, this idea.

Man's relation to nature, in the light of this newer doctrine, thus becomes sufficiently clear. He is not an interloper, but an integral part of a whole. He is the highest outcome (so far as our world of sense is concerned) of a vast upward movement. Nay, modern science links him on to other worlds and other æons. Cosmic evolution is "all of a piece," so to speak, and man takes his own special place in an ordered whole. The process is slow, measured by the standard of human life. Countless ages have lapsed to bring us and our world to its present degree of conscious life. Countless ages are yet to elapse. What shall be the end—the goal ? Who can tell ? Judging by what we know, it would seem simplest to say that

Man and Nature

the trend of the evolutionary process is towards the increase of internal spontaneity and consciously formed and prosecuted purpose. In his " Songs before Sunrise," Swinburne calls this spontaneity " freedom."

> " Freedom we call it, for holier
>   Name of the soul's there is none ;
> Surelier it labours, if slowlier,
>   Than the metres of star and of sun ;
> Slowlier than life unto breath,
> Surelier than time unto death,
>   It moves till its labour is done."

The nature-mystic, then, is bound to reject the " brute " matter doctrine just as decidedly as the doctrine of the unconditioned Absolute. Each, in its own way, robs nature of its true glory and significance. Nature, for him, is living : and that, not indirectly as a " living garment " (to quote Goethe's Time Spirit) of another Reality, but as itself a living part of that Reality—a genuine, primary manifestation of the ultimate Ground. And man is an integral living part of living nature.

There is another aspect of this " brute " matter doctrine which leads to the same conclusions. If matter be held to possess no other properties than those known to the physicist, it might be possible to account for what may be termed the utilitarian side of human development, social and individualistic. Nature makes demands upon man's energies and capacities before she will yield

Nature Mysticism

him food and shelter, and his material requirements generally. The enormously important and far-reaching range of facts here brought to view have largely determined the chequered course of industrial and social evolution. But even so, weighty reservations must be made. There is the element of rationality (implicit in external phenomena) which has responded to the workings of human reason. There are the manifestations of something deeper than physics in the operations of so-called natural laws, and all the moral influences those laws have brought to bear on man's higher development. There is the significant fact that as the resources of civilisation have increased, the pressure of the utilitarian relation has relaxed.

According fullest credit, however, to the influence of the purely " physical " properties of nature, has man no other relation to his external environment than the utilitarian ? The moral influence has been just suggested ; the exploitation of this rich vein has for some time past engaged the attention of evolutionary moralists. Our more immediate concern is with the æsthetic influences. And in nature there is beauty as well as utility. Nor is the beauty a by-product of utility ; it exists on its own account, and asserts itself in its own right. As Emerson puts it—" it is its own excuse for being." As another writer puts it—" in the beauty which we see around us in nature's face, we have felt the smile of a spiritual Being, as

Man and Nature

we feel the smile of our friend adding light and lustre to his countenance." Yes, nature is beautiful and man knows it. How great the number and variety of the emotions and intuitions that beauty can stir and foster will be seen in detail hereafter.

But beauty is not the only agent in moulding and developing man's character. Nature, as will be shown, is a manifestation of immanent ideas which touch life at every point. Ugliness, for example, has its place as well as beauty, and will be dealt with in due course. So with ideas of life and death, of power and weakness, of hope and despondency—these and a thousand others, immanent in external phenomena, have stimulated the powerful imaginations of the infant race, and still maintain their magic to move the sensitive soul. The wonderful mythological systems of the past enshrine science, philosophy, and poetry—and they were prompted by physical phenomena. The philosophy and poetry of the present are still largely dependent on the same phenomena. So it will be to the end.

That the revelation of Reality is a partial one —that the highest summits are veiled in mists— this is freely granted. But the very fact constitutes in itself a special charm. If what we see is so wonderful, what must that be which is behind!

CHAPTER V

MYSTIC RECEPTIVITY

THE general character of the nature-mystic's main contention will now be sufficiently obvious. He maintains that man and his environment are not connected in any merely external fashion, but that they are sharers in the same kind of Being, and therefore livingly related. If this be sound, we shall expect to find that wherever and whenever men are in close and constant touch with nature they will experience some definite sort of influence which will affect their characters and their thoughts. Nor, as will already have been obvious, are we disappointed in this expectation. Let us turn to a somewhat more detailed study of the evidence for the reality and potency of the mystic influence continuously exercised by physical phenomena on man's psychic development.

As has been stated, the nature-mystic lays considerable, though by no means exclusive, stress upon what he calls "intuition." His view of this faculty or capacity is not quite that of the strict psychologist. Herbert Spencer, for instance, in his "Psychology," uses the term intuition in

30

Mystic Receptivity

what he deems to be its " common acceptation "
—" as meaning any cognition reached by an
undecomposable mental act." Of course much
would turn on what is implied by cognition, and
it is impossible to embark on the wide sea of
epistemology, or even on that of the intuitional
controversy, with a view to determining this
point. Spencer's own illustration of an intuited
fact for knowledge—relations which are equal
to the same relation are equal to one another—
would appear to narrow its application to those
so-called self-evident or necessary truths which
are unhesitatingly accepted at first sight. The
nature-mystic, however, while unreservedly re-
cognising this kind of intuition (whatever may be
its origin) demands a wider meaning for the term.
A nearer approach to what he wants is found in
the feats of certain calculating prodigies, who
often seem to reach their astounding results rather
by insights than operations. The celebrated
mathematician, Euler, is said to have possessed,
in addition to his extraordinary memory for
numbers, " a kind of *divining power*," by which
he perceived almost at a glance, the most complicated relations of factors and the best modes of
manipulating them. As regards the calculating
prodigies, a thought suggests itself. It has been
almost invariably found that as they learnt more,
their special power decreased. Has this any bearing on the loss of imaginative power and æsthetic
insight which often accompanies the spread of

Nature Mysticism

civilisation ?—or on the materialisms and the "brute matter" doctrines which so often afflict scientists ?

But even this expansion of meaning does not satisfy the nature-mystic. Perhaps the case of musical intuition comes still nearer to what he is looking for, inasmuch as cognition, in the sense of definite knowledge, is here reduced to a minimum. On the other hand there is more at work than mere feeling. The soul of the music-lover moves about in a world which is at once realised and yet unrealised—his perceptions are vivid and yet indefinable. And it is important to note that the basis is sense-perception.

And thus we say of mystical intuition that it is a passing of the mind, without reasoned process, behind the world of phenomena into a more central sphere of reality—an insight into a world beyond the reach of sense—a direct beholding of spiritual facts, guided by a logic which is implicit, though it does not emerge into consciousness. It is intuition of this fuller and deeper kind which in all likelihood forms the core of what some would call the æsthetic and the moral senses.

And here an interesting question presents itself. The older mystics, and the more orthodox of modern mystics, would have us believe that the intuition for which they contend is purely passive. The mind must be quieted, the will negated, until a state of simple receptivity is attained. Is this contention valid ? It is difficult to break away

32

Mystic Receptivity

from venerable traditions, but the nature-mystic who would be abreast of the knowledge of his day must at times be prepared to submit even intuition itself to critical analysis. And in this instance, criticism is all the more necessary because the doctrine of pure passivity is largely a corollary of belief in an unconditioned Absolute. If union with such an Absolute is to be enjoyed, the will must be pulseless, the intellect atrophied, the whole soul inactive : otherwise the introduction of finite thoughts and desires inhibits the divine afflatus !

Now it was noted, when intuition was first mentioned, that, like sensation (which is an elementary form of intuition) it provides " matter " for the mind to work upon. So far, it may rightly be deemed passive—receptive. But only half the story is thus told. The mind reacts upon the " matter " so provided, and gives it context and meaning. Even the sense-organ reacts to the physical stimulus, and conditions it in its own fashion ; much more will the mind as a whole assert itself. Indeed it is only on condition of such action and reaction that any union, or communion, worthy of the name, can be effected. And should it be suspected that the distinction between " matter " and " form " is too Kantian and technical (though it is not intended to be such) the matter can be stated in more general terms by saying that in all forms of intuition, from the lowest to the highest, the mind goes out to meet that which

D 33

comes to it—there is always some movement from within, be it desire, emotion, sympathy, or other like affection. In short, the self, as long as it is a self, can never be purely passive.

Consider from this point of view the following passage from Jefferies. " With all the intensity of feeling which exalted me, all the intense communion I held with the earth, the sun and sky, the stars hidden by the light, with the ocean—in no manner can the thrilling depth of these feelings be written—with these I prayed, as if they were the keys of an instrument, of an organ, with which I swelled forth the notes of my soul, redoubling my own voice by their power. The great sun burning with light; the strong earth, dear earth; the warm sky; the pure air; the thought of ocean; the inexpressible beauty of all filled me with a rapture, an ecstasy, an inflatus. With this inflatus, too, I prayed." How strong throughout the activity of the soul—culminating in prayer! And by " prayer," Jefferies distinctly states that he means, not " a request for anything preferred to a deity," but intense soul-emotion, intense aspiration, intense desire for fuller soul-life— all the marks of the highest forms of mysticism, and proportionately strengthened soul-activities.

And what, then, shall be said of Wordsworth ?

> " I deem that there are Powers
> Which of themselves our minds impress ;
> That we can feed these minds of ours
> In a wise passiveness.

34

Mystic Receptivity

" Think you, 'mid all this mighty sum
    Of things for ever speaking,
' That nothing of itself will come,
    But we must still be seeking."

Is not this, it may be asked, in harmony with the
older doctrine ? Not so. There is a rightful and
wholesome insistence on the necessity for a receptive attitude of mind. Jefferies, too, was intensely
receptive as well as intensely active. But Wordsworth is contrasting concentration of the mind on
definite studies and on book-lore with the laying
of it open to the influences of nature. He calls
this latter a " wise passiveness "—a " dreaming " :
but is nevertheless an active passivity—a waking dream. All the senses are to be in healthy
working order ; a deep consciousness is to be
gently playing over the material which nature
so spontaneously supplies. And so it comes that
he can tell of

> " A Presence that disturbs me with the joy
>   Of elevated thoughts."

Is not this the same experience as that of Jefferies,
only passing through a mind of calmer tone. And
if at times Wordsworth also is lifted into an
ecstasy, when

> " the light of sense
> Goes out, but with a flash that has revealed
> The invisible world,"

his mind is not in an Absolutist state of passivity,
but, on the contrary, is stirred to higher forms of

35

consciousness. The experiences may, or may not be such as subsequent reflection can reduce to order—that is immaterial to the issue—but at any rate they imply activity. We may safely conclude, therefore, that intuition in all its grades necessitates a specialised soul-activity as well as a specialised soul-passivity.

It will have been apparent in what has preceded that there are many grades of intuition, rising from sense-perception to what is known as ecstasy. Some may doubt the wisdom of admitting ecstasy among the experiences of a sane, modern nature-mystic. Certainly the word raises a prejudice in many minds. Certainly the fanaticisms of religious Mysticism must be avoided. But Jefferies was not frightened of the word to describe an unwonted experience of exalted feeling; nor was Wordsworth afraid to describe the experience itself :

> " that serene and blessed mood
> In which the affections gently lead us on—
> Until the breath of this corporeal flame, _frame ?_
> And even the motion of our human blood
> Almost suspended, we are laid asleep
> In body, and become a living soul ;
> While with an eye made quiet by the power
> Of harmony, and the deep power of joy,
> We see into the life of things."

This is in many respects the same type of experience as that described by Plotinus—"the life of the gods, and of divine and happy men "—but shorn of its needless degradation of the body

Mystic Receptivity

and the senses, which, with Wordsworth are still and transcended, but remain as a foundation for all the rest. There is yet another and very significant point of difference. Porphyry, a disciple of Plotinus, tells us that his master attained to the ecstatic condition four times only in the six years which he spent in his company. How often Wordsworth attained to his form of ecstasy we do not know. But there is the little word "we" which occurs throughout his description : and this evidently links the past on to his readers. That is to say, he does not sever his experience from that which is open to ordinary humanity. He called for and anticipated genuine sympathy. Nor was he wrong in making this demand, for there are few sensitive lovers of nature who are not able to parallel, in some degree, what the English high-priest of Nature Mysticism has so wonderfully described. And as for the lower and simpler grades of feeling for nature, given that the conditions of life are "natural," they are practically universal, though often inarticulate.

CHAPTER VI

DEVELOPMENT AND DISCIPLINE OF INTUITION

ALTHOUGH the outstanding mark of intuition is its immediacy, that does not imply that it is independent of mental development, of culture, or of discipline. So far all classes of mystics would be agreed. Nevertheless a certain amount of comment and criticism will be useful even in this regard. For erroneous conceptions, especially in matters so largely influenced by belief in an unconditioned Absolute, may frequently issue in harmful practices. For proof and illustration of the danger, need one do more than point to the terrible excesses of asceticism still prevalent in India?

And first, of the normal development of the mystic feeling for nature in the case of the individual mind. "The child is father of the man," said Wordsworth. But in what sense is this true? Let us turn to the immortal Ode, which is undoubtedly a record of vivid personal experience.

" Heaven lies about us in our infancy !
  Shades of the prison-house begin to close
        Upon the growing boy,
  But he beholds the light and whence it flows,
        He sees it in his joy ;

38

Development and Discipline

The youth who daily farther from the east
Must travel, still is Nature's priest,
    And by the vision splendid
    Is on his way attended;
At length the man perceives it die away
And fade into the light of common day."

Of course the poet was in dead earnest in writing thus; but the two last lines give us pause. How about

"The light that never was on land or sea"?

Was not that with the poet to the end? How about the

"Thoughts that do often lie too deep for tears"?

Would those have been possible for the child or growing boy? If there had been a loss, had there not also been a very real gain as the years rolled over his head? Such questions are forced upon us by an examination of the records themselves. Somewhat of the brightness and freshness of "the vision splendid" might evaporate; but the mystic glow, the joy, the exaltation, remained—and deepened—

"So was it when I was a child,
So is it now I am a man,
So may it be when I am old,
    Or let me die"—

only that childlike fancy yields place to matured imagination. And if this was so with Wordsworth, whose childhood was so exceptional, still more shall we find it to be true of the average child. The

39

Nature Mysticism

early freshness of the senses may be blunted ; the eager curiosity may be satiated ; but where the nature remains unspoilt, the sense of wonder and of joy will extend its range and gain in fullness of content.

If we compare Kingsley's development, he was in a way a great " boy " to the end—but a boy with a deepening sense of mystery mellowing his character and his utterances. And thus it was that he could say, looking back on his intercourse with the wonders of nature : " I have long enjoyed them, never I can honestly say alone, because when man was not with me I had companions in every bee and flower and pebble, and never idle, because I could not pass a swamp or a tuft of heather without finding in it a fairy tale of which I could but decipher here and there a line or two, and yet found them more interesting than all the books, save one, which were ever written upon earth."

True, there is another range of experiences to be reckoned with, such as that of Omar Khayyám—

" Yet ah that Spring should vanish with the Rose !
That Youth's sweet-scented manuscript should close !
The Nightingale that on the branches sang,
Ah whence, and whither flown again, who knows ? "

Yes, but what might Omar have been with a nobler philosophy of life, and a more wholesome self-restraint. Blasé, toper as he was, how did he begin his Rubáiyát ? Thus finely !

Development and Discipline

> "Wake! For the Sun who scatter'd into flight
> The stars before him from the Field of Night,
> Drives Night along with them from Heav'n and strikes
> The Sultan's turret with a Shaft of Light."

There was poetry in the man still—and that, too, of the kind stirred by nature. And from nature likewise comes the pathos of a closing verse—

> "Yon rising Moon that looks for us again—
> How oft hereafter will she wax and wane;
> How oft hereafter rising look for us
> Through this same Garden—and for *one* in vain!"

And if in spite of all that is said, Wordsworth's haunting Ode still asserts its sway, then let there be a still more direct appeal to its author. One of his loveliest sonnets is that which opens—

> "It is a beauteous evening, calm and free."

He tells of the holy stillness, the setting of the broad sun, the eternal motion of the sea. He is filled with a sense of mystic adoration. And then there is a sudden turn of thought—

> "Dear child! dear girl! that walkest with me here,
> If thou appear untouch'd by solemn thought,
> Thy nature is not therefore less divine."

What is this but to regard the intuitional faculty as still largely latent, awaiting the maturing processes of the passing years? There is no place for further argument.

What has just been said of the child may be

41

Nature Mysticism

said of the race, especially if there is anything
in the theory that the child recapitulates in brief
the stages through which the race has passed in its
upward progress. In the dawn of civilisation the
senses would be comparatively fresh and keen,
though lacking in delicacy of æsthetic discrimination; the imagination would be powerful and
active. Hence the products, so varied and immense, of the animistic tendency and the mythopœic faculty. To these stages succeed the periods
of reflective thought and accurate research, which,
while blunting to some degree the sharp edge of
sensibility, more than atone for the loss by the
widening of horizons and the deepening of mysteries. We must be careful, however, not to press
the analogy, or parallel, too far. Important modifications of the recapitulation theory are being urged
even on its biological side; it is wise, therefore,
to be doubly on guard when dealing with the complexities of social development. Still, it is safe
to assert that, for the race as for the individual,
the modes of cosmic emotion grow fuller and
richer in " the process of the suns." Would it be
easy to parallel in any previous period of history
that passage from Jefferies?—" With all the intensity of feeling which exalted me, all the intense
communion I held with the earth, the sun, and
the sky, the stars hidden by the light, with the
ocean—in no manner can the thrilling depth of
these feelings be written—with these I prayed, as
if they were the keys of an instrument."

42

Development and Discipline

Starting from an acknowledgment that the intuitional faculty is capable of development, it is an easy, and indeed inevitable, step to the conclusion that training and discipline can aid that development. As noted above, mystics have gone, and still go, to lengths which make the world wonder, in their efforts to enjoy the higher forms of mystic communion with the Real. The note of stern renunciation has persisted like a bourdon down the ages in the lives of those who have devoted themselves to the quest of the Absolute. In the East, and more especially in India, the grand aim of life has come to be the release from the appetites and the senses. The Buddhist struggles to suppress all natural desires, and undergoes all manner of self-inflicted tortures, that he may rise above the world of illusion, and attain to absorption in the Universal Spirit. He sacrifices the body that the soul may see. Similar views, though varying much in detail, have flourished at the heart of all the great religions, and have formed almost the sole substance of some of the smaller. Nor has Christianity escaped. An exaggerated and uncompromising asceticism has won for many Christian saints their honours on earth and their assurance of special privileges in heaven.

Contrast with this sterner and narrower type, the mystic who loves the natural world because he believes it to be, like himself, a genuine manifestation of the ultimately Real, and to be akin to his own inmost life. He, too, acknowledges the need

43

Nature Mysticism

for the discipline of the body—he, too, has his *askesis*—but he cherishes the old Greek ideal which does not call for a sacrifice of sense as such, but for a wise abstinence from those sensual pleasures, or over-indulgences in pleasure, which endanger the balance of the powers of the body and the mind. The nature-mystic, more particularly, maintains that there is no form of human knowledge which may not be of service to him in attaining to deeper insight and fuller experience in his intercourse with nature. He is therefore a student, in the best sense of the word—not a slave to mere erudition, but an alert and eager absorber of things new and old according to his abilities and opportunities. He tries to survey life as a whole, and to bring his complete self, body and soul, to the realisation of its possibilities. And he looks to nature for some of his purest joys and most fruitful experiences. He knows that the outward shows of heaven and earth are manifestations of a Reality which communes with him as soul with soul.

CHAPTER VII

NATURE NOT SYMBOLIC

MYSTICISM and symbolism are generally regarded as inseparable : some may go so far as to make them practically synonymous. Hence the large space devoted to symbols in most treatises on Mysticism. Récéjac, for instance, in his treatise on the " Bases of the Mystic Belief," devotes about two-thirds of the whole to this subject. Whence such preponderating emphasis ? There are, of course, many conspiring causes, but the conception of the Absolute is still the strongest. Given an Unconditioned which is beyond the reach of sense and reason, the phenomenal is necessarily degraded to the rank of the merely symbolical. Nature, being at an infinite distance from the Real, can only " stand for " the Real ; and any knowledge which it can mediate is so indirect as to be hardly worthy of the name.

To this degradation of the phenomenal the true nature-mystic is bound to demur, if he is to be faithful to his fundamental principle. He desires direct communion with the Real, and looks to external nature as a means to attain his end. To palm off upon him something which " stands

45

Nature Mysticism

for " the Real is to balk him of his aim; for the moment the symbol appears, the Real disappears : its place is taken by a substitute which at the best is Mâya—an illusion; or, to use technical phraseology of the metaphysical sort, is " mere appearance."

But further, the symbolic conception of nature would seem to contradict the requirement of immediacy—a requirement more vital to the Absolutist than to the genuine nature-mystic, and yet apparently lost from the view of those who are the strongest advocates of symbolism. For intuition implies direct insight, independent of reasoning process and conceptual construction. Whereas, a symbol, in any ordinary acceptation of the word, is indisputably a product of conscious mental processes : its very reference beyond itself demands conscious analysis and synthesis, and a conscious recognition of complicated systems of relations. The doctrine of symbols is thus in reality subversive of Mysticism of any kind, and more especially of Nature Mysticism.

Let it not be supposed that to argue thus is to repudiate symbolism as such. Whoever understands the nature and conditions of human knowledge sees that symbolic systems, of endless variety, are necessary instruments in almost every department of theory, research, and practice. We cannot move without them. Some symbols are thoroughly abstract and artificial, but frequently of the utmost value, in spite of their being

Nature not Symbolic

pure creations of the mind. Other symbols are founded on analogies and affinities deep down in the nature of things, and so come nearer to the matter of genuine intuition. Between the two extremes there are an infinite number of graded systems, some of which enter into the very texture of daily life. But so long as, and in so far as, there is a " standing for " instead of a " being," the mystic, quâ mystic, is defrauded of his direct communion with the Ground of things.

But the mystic who champions symbolism may object that the definition of that term must not be taken so narrowly, and that there is the wider sense in which it is taken by writers on æsthetics. Some such definition as this may be attempted: A symbol is something which does not merely " stand for " something else, but one which, while it has a meaning of its own, points onward to another thing beyond itself, and suggests an ideal content which of itself it cannot fully embody. But are we really cleared of our difficulty by substituting " suggests " for " stands for " ? Again it must be insisted that the mystic aims at direct communion, not with that which is " suggested," but that which " is." An object may be low or high in the scale of existence, may be rich or poor in content—but it is what it is, and, as such, and in and for itself, may be the source of an intuition. The man lying on the bank of the mill-stream and meditating on the water-wheel wanted the secret of the wheel itself, not what the wheel " sug-

Nature Mysticism

gested." Jefferies, yearning for fuller soul-life, and sensitive to nature's aspects, felt that the life was there—that the universe *is* the life—that the life is intuited in and through the universe, though not grasped as yet by the conscious reasoning processes.

As an interesting example, the symbol of the cross may be briefly considered. Why should a form so simple and so familiar have acquired an astonishingly wide range and be generally regarded as symbolic of life? Much has to be learnt before the problem is solved. One thing seems fairly certain—the choice has not been wholly arbitrary; there has been at work an intuitional, subconscious factor. Is it possible that the negativing of a line in one direction by a line in another direction raises subliminally a sense of strain, then of effort, then of purposeful will, and so, lastly, of life? Probably a piece of pure imagination! And yet there must be some real power in the symmetrical form itself to account for its symbolic career. Conscious reason, obscurely prompted by this power, evolved the symbolic use; and the strange interminglings of intuition, rational action, and force of circumstance, during the long course of civilised history, have accomplished the rest.

The train of reflection thus started will add special point to a passage from an early letter of Kingsley's, quoted by Inge in a slightly curtailed form, but here given in full. " The great Mysticism

Nature not Symbolic

is the belief that is becoming every day stronger
with me, that all symmetrical natural objects, aye,
and perhaps all forms, colours, and scents which
show organisation or arrangement, are types of
some truth or existence, of a grade between the
symbolical type and the mystic type. When I
walk the fields I am oppressed every now and then
with an innate feeling, that everything I see has a
meaning, if I could but understand it. And this
feeling of being surrounded with truths which I
cannot grasp, amounts to indescribable awe sometimes ! Everything seems to be full of God's
reflex, if we could but see it."

The passage is of profound significance when
taken as a whole, and will serve as a remarkable
description of the genuine mystic experience which
can be prompted by nature, without going to the
length of " vision," still less of ecstasy. But the
stress now lies on the words—" a grade between
the symbolical type and the mystic type."
Kingsley evidently realised the insufficiency of
symbolism to meet his demands, while he shrank
from the vagueness of what was called Mysticism.
Objects for him had a meaning in their own right,
and he was casting about for a fitting term to express this fact. He also distinctly states that to
him, " Everything seems to be full of God's
reflex." Once grant that Nature Mysticism, as
defined and illustrated in the preceding chapters,
is a genuine form of Mysticism, and his difficulty
would be solved. The natural objects which

Nature Mysticism

stirred his emotions would be acknowledged as part and parcel of the ultimate Ground itself, and therefore competent to act, not as substitutes for something else not really present, but in their own right, and of their own sovereign prerogative. Nature, in short, is not a mere stimulus for a roving fancy or teeming imagination : it is a power to be experienced, a secret to be wrested, a life to be shared.

The famous " Canticle of the Sun " of St. Francis d'Assisi gives naïve and spontaneous expression to the same truth. Natural objects, for this purest of mystics, were no bare symbols, nor did they gain their significance by suggesting beyond themselves. He addressed them as beings who shared with him the joy of existence. " My Brother the Sun " — " my Sister the Moon " — " our Mother the Earth " — " my Brother the Wind " — " our Sister Water " — " Brother Fire." The same form of address is maintained for things living and things lifeless. And it is obvious that the endearing terms of relationship are more than metaphors or figures of speech. His heart evidently goes with them : he genuinely claims kinship. Differences dissolve in a sense of common being. It would be an anachronism to read into these affectionate names the more fully developed mysticism of Blake, or Shelley, or Emerson. But the absence of any tinge of symbolic lore is noteworthy.

Kingsley, as was just seen, was feeling about

50

Nature not Symbolic

for something more satisfactory than mystic
symbolism ; so also was Emerson. "Mysticism"
(he writes) "consists in the mistake of an accidental and individual symbol for an universal
one. . . . The mystic must be steadily told, 'All
that you say is just as true without the tedious
use of that symbol as with it.'" Emerson's un-
easiness is manifest. He is rebelling, but is not
quite sure of his ground. At one time he inclines
to think the mystic in fault because he "nails a
symbol to one sense, which was a true sense for
a moment, but soon becomes old and false." At
another time he is inclined to condemn the symbol
altogether as being of too "accidental" a character.
But it is surely simpler to throw symbolism overboard so far as genuine mystic experience is concerned. What the mystic is in search of is
"meaning" in its own right—"meaning" existing
in and for itself. Anything less is a fraud. Emerson nearly reached this conclusion, as witness the
following passage : "A happy symbol is a sort of
evidence that your thought is just. . . . If you
agree with me, or if Locke or Montesquieu agree,
I may yet be wrong ; but if the elm tree thinks the
same thing, if running water, if burning coal, if
crystals, if alkalies, in their several fashions, say
what I say, it must be true." Here Emerson is all
but clean out of the tangle. He speaks of a
"happy symbol." But inasmuch as this "happy
symbol" is to express what the elm tree, the
running water, and the rest, *actually say* in their

51

Nature Mysticism

several fashions, it is safer to drop the idea of symbolism altogether; for what they *say*, is not what they " stand for," but what they actually *are*.

If the contention is renewed that the elm tree, running water, and the rest, *suggest* truths and thoughts beyond themselves, of course the point may be readily granted. But this is only to affirm that every object is linked on to every other object by a multiplicity of relations—that each part is woven into the texture of a larger whole in a universe of interpenetrations. The consistent working out of the organic interdependence of the modes and forms of existence is found in such a system as that of Hegel, where each part pre-supposes correlatives, and where each stage or " moment " includes all the past, and presses on to that which dialectically succeeds. It is not necessary to be a Hegelian to appreciate the grand idea of his doctrine—that all modes and manifestations of the Real are logically and organically connected. But to say that one stage of the evolution of the Idea is dependent on another, or essentially involves another, is not to make the lower of the stages symbolic of the higher. Indeed to introduce the concept of symbolism at all into such a context is to court inextricable confusion. Let symbolism be one thing, and let organic (or dialectic) connection be another—then we know where we are when we claim for natural objects that they have a

Nature not Symbolic

being and a meaning in their own right, and that
they are akin to the soul of man. Emerson had
a firm grasp of the nature-mystic's inevitable contention.

> " The rounded world is fair to see,
>   Nine-times folded in mystery :
>   Though baffled seers cannot impart
>   The secret of its labouring heart.
>   Throb thine with Nature's throbbing breast,
>   And all is clear from east to west.
>   Spirit that lurks each form within
>   Beckons to spirit of its kin ;
>   Self-kindled every atom glows,—
>   And hints the future which it owes."

CHAPTER VIII

THE CHARGE OF ANTHROPOMORPHISM

THERE are many thinkers who are ready to acknowledge that the contemplation of nature leads to various kinds of emotional and æsthetic experience, but who at the same time deny that the results of such contemplation have any other than a subjective character; they argue that the validity of the results evaporates, so to speak, with the mood which brought them into being. Myths, for example, from this point of view are " simply the objectification of subjective impulses "; and modern sympathy with nature is æsthetic feeling which " breaks free of the fetters laid upon it by mythological thought, constantly to create at its own sovereign pleasure myths which pass with the passing of the end that they have served and give place to other fancies." This " subjective " doctrine will meet us often, and will call for various answers. Let it now be considered in its most general and formidable shape, that to which Wundt has given weighty support in his treatise on the " Facts of the Moral Life." The sentences quoted just above are from those sections of this work which deal with man's æsthetic relation to

54

nature; and it is with their teaching on the subject that this chapter will be chiefly concerned.

Here is a statement which raises a clear issue. The influence of nature, says Wundt, is not immutable. " The same mountains and rivers and forests lie before the modern European that lay before his ancestors thousands of years ago ; but the effect which they produce is very different. In this change there is reflected a change in man's *æsthetic* view of the world, itself connected with a change in his moral apprehension of life." Now every word of this passage may be welcomed by the nature-mystic without his thereby yielding his contention that mountains and rivers and forests have a definite and immanent objective significance of their own. The phenomena of sunrise and sunset, which lay before our European ancestors thousands of years ago, are the same as those which present themselves to the modern astronomer, and yet how differently interpreted ! Does the difference imply that the early observer had no objective facts before him, and that modern astronomy has advanced to a freedom which enables it to frame hypotheses at its sovereign will ? Such a conclusion is just possible as we meditate on the mutability of many scientific concepts ! Still, the conclusion would be regarded as somewhat violent. But if it is allowed that in the latter case, the basis of objective fact gives continuity to the development of astronomic lore,

Nature Mysticism

why should the same privilege not be accorded to the objective element in the continuity of mystical lore ? As knowledge grows, interpretations become more adequate to the objective facts, but it does not negate them. And Wundt himself allows that " it is from the mythological form of the feeling (for nature), which reaches back to the first beginnings of human civilisation, that the æsthetic feeling for nature with which we are ourselves familiar has been slowly and gradually evolved." How could such continuity be secured without some basis in the world of fact ?

And the basis in fact is surely easy of discovery. Man is not a solitary being, suspended between earth and heaven. On the contrary, he is related to all below him and all that is above him by 'ties which enter into the very fibre of his being. He is himself a child of nature, nurtured on the bosom of Mother Earth and raising his eyes to the height of the Empyrean. Evolution, whatever it may be, is a cosmic process—and man is a link in a chain, or rather, a living member of a living universe. For an evolutionist to argue man's relation to his physical environment to be external in its physical aspects would be deemed arrant folly. Is it less foolish for an evolutionist to isolate man's emotions, feelings, and thoughts ?

" In proportion " (says Wundt) " as nature lost her immediate and living reality " (by the passing of mythology) " did the human mind possess itself of her, to find its own subjective states

The Charge of Anthropomorphism

reflected in her features." Much obviously turns
on the implications of the word " reflected." We
are led to hope much when he speaks of " the
kinship of the emotions set up by certain phenomena
of nature with moods arising from within "—but
he empties his statement of mystic meaning by
adding, " at the mind's own instance." " Nature "
(says Auerbach in plainer terms) " has no moods,
they belong to man alone." Tennyson gives
expression to this view (not on his own behalf !) :

> " all the phantom, Nature, stands,
>   With all the music in her tone
> A hollow echo of my own—
>   A hollow form with empty hands."

But surely all this negation of moods in nature,
this determination to empty natural phenomena
of all definite human significance, is invalidated
by one very simple consideration. There must be
some correspondence between cause and effect.
When certain moods are stimulated by certain
physical phenomena, there must be *some* sort of
real causation. It is not *any* scene that can har-
monise with or foster *any* mood. The range of
variety in the effects produced by mountains,
rivers, sunsets, and the rest, is admittedly great,
but it is not chaotic. The nature-mystic admits
variety, nay, rejoices in it, but he postulates an
equivalent variety of influences immanent in the
phenomena. Of course Auerbach is right if by
mood in nature he means an experience similar to

57

Nature Mysticism

that of the human observer: but he is wrong if he implies that the mood is wholly a subjective creation, and that the object, or group of objects, which stimulates the mood has no quality or power which corresponds to, or is essentially connected with, the mood.

Turner's famous "Fighting Téméraire" combines into an exquisite whole a group of human moods and natural phenomena. Was his choice of phenomena determined by purely subjective considerations? A veteran warship is being towed by a little steamer to her last berth. The human interest is intense. The problem is to give it a fitting and noble setting. Study the nature-setting which the artist has chosen for his theme— the wealth of glowing, but gently subdued colour —the sun setting, like the old ship, in mellow glory—the crescent moon that speaks of the birth of a new economic era—the cool mists stealing up, precursors of the night when work is done—how marvellously all these tone with the general sentiment. Shall it be maintained that they are arbitrary conventions, mere fanciful products of the association of ideas? Armed with triple brass must be the breast of the critic who could uphold such a view. For the common heart of humanity repudiates it, and intuitively feels that in such a picture there is more than a display of artistic skill embodying subtle symbols —it feels that there is a blending of elements which share a common spiritual nature.

58

The Charge of Anthropomorphism

The same conclusion is reached when the matter is brought to the test of science and philosophy. Science, in its own domain, is every whit as anthropomorphic as Nature Mysticism—and inevitably so if it is to exist at all; for it rests upon the assumption that the behaviour of external objects is in harmony with the workings of human reason. In other words, it postulates a vital relationship between man's inner nature and the inner nature of his material environment. Human reason goes out into nature expecting to find there something akin to itself, and is not disappointed of its hope. Man's conceptions of this kinship were at first, like all his other conceptions, crude and confused; but as his experience widened and ripened, his outlook became more adequate to the infinite complexity and variety of the phenomena with which he has to deal. And throughout, both in the lower and in the higher stages of intellectual development, the same truth unchangingly asserts itself, that man is a microcosm. His reason proves it by finding itself in the macrocosm. And what holds good of the imperfect and recently developed rational faculties holds good even more substantially of the fundamental instincts and emotions, and of intuitions and spiritual promptings.

The scientist of a materialistic bent may here object that as the sphere of human knowledge extends it becomes increasingly evident that all the operations in the universe are under the sway

59

of inexorable laws. The issues thus raised are obviously too large to be discussed at any length in the present context. But two observations of a general character will serve to indicate that there are weighty counter-considerations. The first is that the human heart rebels against the conception of a mechanically determined universe while conceiving itself a product of, or integral part of, that universe. That is to say, we reject the strange theory of a mechanical universe rebelling against itself! Some of the inexorable laws must, to say the least, be of a very different character from that which the scientist postulates! The second consideration is almost a corollary of the first, but also occupies new ground. These "laws" which are so indefatigably hurled at us —what are they? Who can say? Even in their simplest manifestations they pass out of our ken. The most fundamental of them all, from the scientific point of view—the law of the conservation of energy—is now being openly questioned. Much more is there uncertainty as to the laws of life, and the obscure trends and impulses grouped under the head of evolution. So strongly does the stream of criticism bear upon the foundations of the house of the physical scientist, that the old temptation to hasty, and sometimes arrogant, dogmatism is rapidly disappearing. The knowledge of "laws" still leaves, and ever will leave, ample breathing room for the poet, the artist, the nature-mystic, and the soul that loves.

The Charge of Anthropomorphism

There is, however, another aspect of the charge of anthropomorphism—one which is more difficult to deal with because it affects at times the nature-mystic himself. In attempting to deal with it, it will be well to let representative thinkers put their own case. Jefferies, for example, writes thus: "There is nothing human in nature. The earth, though loved so dearly, would let me perish on the ground, and neither bring forth food nor water. Burning in the sky, the great sun, of whose company I have been so fond, would merely burn on and make no motion to assist me. . . . As for the sea, it offers us salt water which we cannot drink. The trees care nothing for us ; the hill I visited so often in days gone by has not missed me. . . . There is nothing human in the whole round of nature. All nature, all the universe that we can see, is absolutely indifferent to us, and except to us human life is of no more value than grass."

Now what does the charge, as thus stated, really amount to? There is no implication that nature is hostile, as some (perhaps including Huxley) would have us think. There is simply a feeling that nature is remote from human modes of experience, indifferent to human interests. And it would be puerile to dispute the rightness of this impression so long as the standpoint of the individual human being is adopted. The individual man is a centre of self-consciousness in a peculiar sense. He has numberless and interminable par-

61

Nature Mysticism

ticular wants, hopes, fears, pleasures, pains. Whereas, the infra-human objects in nature have not attained to his particular mode of consciousness : theirs differs from his in degree, perchance in kind. A tree, a cloud, a mountain, a wave—these cannot enter into what we call "personal" relations with each other or with human beings. But this is not to say that they may not possess a consciousness, which though different from man's consciousness, is yet akin to it and linked to it. Nay, the nature-mystic's experiences, as well as the metaphysician's speculations, declare that the linking up must be regarded as a fact. And when we examine more carefully what Jefferies says, we find that he in no way disputes this fact. How could it be, with his vivid sense of communion with forms of being still more remote from the human than the sea-monsters he names ? What oppressed him was a feeling of strangeness. In other words, nature was "remote" for him because he felt he did not understand it well enough.

Further discussion of the important issues thus raised will be postponed until certain forms of modern animism come under review. One or two preliminary observations, however, will be in place at this earlier stage. It is wise, for example, not to forget the limitations of our knowledge. A platitude ! Yes—but one which even the greatest thinkers are apt to lose sight of, with consequent tendency to hasty generalisation and

The Charge of Anthropomorphism

undue neglect of deep-seated instincts and intuitions. The discovery of some new cosmic law
may change the whole face of nature, and set in a
new light its apparent remoteness or indifference.
Again, as has just been shown, natural phenomena
are in definite relationship to human reason.
They are comprehensible—therefore not alien.
By their aid we can organise our conduct, and
even our ideals—therefore they are factors in
our self-realisation. Thus, underlying their seeming indifference, it is possible even now to trace
their beneficent influences in the evolutionary
process. And since they embody reason, beauty,
and goodness, we can afford to await in patience
the solution of many problems which trouble us,
and surrender ourselves trustfully to the calm,
resistless forces which are weaving the web of
cosmic destinies.

A fine example of the trustful attitude is found
in an article of Lord Dunraven's describing his
life in the woods of New Brunswick: "The earth
sleeps. A silence that can be felt has fallen over
the woods. The stars begin to fade. A softer
and stronger light wells up and flows over the
scene as the broad moon slowly floats above the
tree tops. . . . The tree trunks stand out distinct
in the lessening gloom; the dark pine boughs
overhead seem to stoop caressingly towards you.
Amid a stillness that is terrifying, man is not
afraid. Surrounded by a majesty that is appal-
ling, he shrinks not nor is he dismayed. In a

63

Nature Mysticism

scene of utter loneliness he feels himself not to be alone. A sense of companionship, a sensation of satisfaction, creep over him. He feels at one with Nature, at rest in her strong protecting arms."

There is no need, then, to be afraid of a charge of anthropomorphism, if only our conceptions of nature do not lag behind our clear knowledge of its forms and forces. Man, being what he is, is, of course, compelled to think as man and to speak as man ; he cannot jump off his own shadow. But since he is himself part and parcel of the cosmos, his thinking and speaking are *within*, not external to, the material cosmos. So completely is he within, that his knowledge of himself comes to him only by seeing himself reflected in the greater whole. And thus, provided we are true to the highest principles we have attained, we shall be safer when we look out on nature with the analogy of human agency in our mind, than when we regard its course as alien and indifferent. In other words, Nature is not merely an Æolian harp which re-echoes tones given out by the human soul—though that would be much !—but an indispensable agent in producing them. The action is reciprocal, just because man and his external world interpenetrate at every point, and are united organically in a common life.

CHAPTER IX

THE IMMANENT IDEA

So much by way of direct answer to the formidable attack upon the nature-mystic's position. In turning to more constructive work, which will furnish many indirect answers, it will be necessary to take another brief but exhilarating plunge into metaphysics.

We found that external objects somehow, through sensations, obtain admission into the mind, and become part of its possessions in the form of experience. Intuition of various grades is at the base of all mental development. Reflective thought goes to work on the material thus provided, and weaves certain portions of it into the structure of systematised knowledge. Much of it, however, never emerges into clear consciousness—it is felt rather than known—sometimes not even felt, though it influences the mind, affects its mood or tone, and largely moulds its character and the products of its more conscious processes. Intuition thus contains implicitly what reflection and reason strive to render explicit.

It will be remembered that, in the first chapter, the metaphysical theory broadly adopted was that

Nature Mysticism

which may be called Ideal-Realism. The distinctive teaching is that while Materialism stops short at external objects which can resist, and while Subjective Idealism stops short at the perceiving mind, Ideal-Realism affirms the reality of objects and perceiving mind alike, but regards them as mutually dependent, and as fused in the activity of consciousness. Can the conclusions just summed up and the metaphysical theory adopted be brought into helpful connection ?

Yes, if the human mind and the external world are made of the same stuff—if the mind is invisible nature, and nature visible mind. For Materialism cannot bridge the gap between matter and consciousness ; Subjective Idealism can never move out into a real world. But if nature and mind are genuinely akin, as the nature-mystic holds, there is no gap to bridge, no mind condemned to hopeless isolation. Nature is then seen to be a manifestation of the same mental factors which we discover when we analyse our inner experience— namely, consciousness, feeling, will, and reason. The nature-mystic's communion with the external world takes its place as a valid mode of realising the essential sameness of all forms of existences and of all cosmic activities. Science is another such valid mode, art another, philosophy another, religion yet another—none of them ultimately antagonistic, but mutually supplementary. Some mystics will say that the union of man with nature is actually at any moment complete, but has to be

66

The Immanent Idea

brought into the light of conscious experience. Other mystics, who hold dualistic, pluralistic, or pragmatic views, will maintain that the union may assume ever new forms and develop ever new potentialities. But such differences are subsidiary, and cannot obscure the fundamental doctrine on which all consistent nature-mystics must be agreed, that man and nature are essentially manifestations of the same Reality.

It is deeply significant to note that, at the very dawn of reflective thought, a conviction of the essential sameness of all existence seized upon the minds of the fathers of Western philosophy, and dominated their speculations. The teaching of these bold pioneers was inevitably coloured and limited by their social environment; but it was also so shot through with flashes of intuition and acute reasonings, that it anticipated many of the latest developments of modern research. A study of its main features will occupy us at a later stage, when we come to deal with certain of nature's most striking phenomena. The simple fact is here emphasised that the earliest effort of human reflective thought was to discover the *Welt-stoff*—the substance which underlies all modes and forms of existence, and that man was regarded as an integral and organic part of the whole.

Greek philosophy, which started with these crude, but brilliant speculations, had developed a wonderful variety and subtlety, when Plato, animated by the same desire to discover the

Nature Mysticism

Ground of things, introduced his doctrine of Ideas. He held that bodies are not, in themselves, the true reality; they are manifestations of something else. Reality, for him, is a system of real thoughts which he calls Ideas, and the world of objects gets its reality by participating in them or by copying them. The senses, under such conditions, cleave to the copies, whereas the mind, in thinking by general ideas, apprehends the true reality. These ideas must not be regarded as mere products of the mind, but as real existences, which, when manifested under conditions of time and space, multiply themselves in innumerable objects. In fact, so real are they that without them there would be no objects at all.

Schopenhauer adopted this doctrine of Ideas, and brought it into connection with his characteristic theory of Will as the ultimate Ground. The Ideas, for him, represent definite forms of existence, manifested in individual things and beings. There are thus, he said, Ideas of the simple elementary forces of nature, such as gravity and impenetrability; there are Ideas of the different forms of individual things; and there are Ideas of the different species of organic beings, including man. He followed Plato in refusing any true reality to individual objects and separated the Idea from its sensuous form. "By Idea, then" (he writes), "I understand every definite and fixed grade of the objectification of will, so far as it is a thing-in-itself, and therefore has no

The Immanent Idea

multiplicity. These grades are related to individual things as their eternal forms or prototypes." Hence, the world known to the senses could be nothing other than mere phenomenal appearance.

Now it is manifestly an enormous stride in the direction of Nature Mysticism to recognise in material objects a factor, or element, which is akin to the highest activities of the human mind. But, as already stated, in expounding the view known as Ideal-Realism, the nature-mystic cannot be content to stop here. Nor indeed was Schopenhauer consistent in stopping here. If he had been faithful to his conception of Will as the Ground of all existence, he could not well have denied some degree of reality to objects in their own right. This particular tree, this particular table, this particular cloud—what are they, each in its individual capacity, but objectifications of will?—therefore real! Each individual object is *unique*, and fills a place of its own in the totality of objects—each is related to all the rest in particular and defined manners and degrees—each exhibits a special kind of behaviour in a special environment. Why, then, deny to each individual thing its own grade and degree of reality?

Thus there is in each object an immanent idea; but this is fused with the sensuous form, and presents itself to conscious human thought as an objective manifestation of the Real. There is an organic interpenetration of the sensuous and the

Nature Mysticism

spiritual ; and it is by virtue of this interpenetration that the human reason can go out into the external world and find itself there. As Emerson well puts it—" Nature is the incarnation of thought, and turns to a thought again, as ice becomes water and gas. The world is mind precipitated, and the volatile essence is for ever escaping again into the state of free thought. Hence the virtue and pungency of the influence on the mind, of natural objects, whether inorganic or organised."

The nature-mystic is not without authoritative support, even on the Idealist side, in his demand that individual objects shall be allowed some grade and measure of reality. Spinoza, for instance, allows that each individual thing is a genuine part of the total Idea. Hegel also grants to individual things a certain " self-reference," which constitutes them real existences. The nature-mystic, therefore, may be of good cheer in asserting that even the most transient phenomenon not only "participates" in an immanent Idea, but embodies it, gives it a concrete form and place. He thus substantiates his claim that communion with nature is communion with the Ground of things.

CHAPTER X

ANIMISM, ANCIENT AND MODERN

AFTER this metaphysical bath we return invigorated to the world of concrete experience dear alike to the common-sense thinker and the modern investigator. Do the facts of life, as ordinarily presented, or as systematised in reflection, at all point in the direction of the doctrine of immanent ideas ? It will be seen that this question admits of an affirmative answer. But the term " idea " must be taken as embracing psychic existence in its entirety—that is to say, feeling and will, as well as reason. The dry bones of reason must be clothed with flesh and blood. The appeal is to actual experience. Let Walt Whitman give us his. " Doubtless there comes a time when one feels through his whole being, and pronouncedly the emotional part, that identity between himself subjectively and Nature objectively which Schelling and Fichte are so fond of pressing. How it is I know not, but I often realise a presence here—in clear moods I am certain of it, and neither chemistry nor reasoning, nor æsthetics will give the least explanation."

Walt Whitman mentions Fechner. Here is

71

Nature Mysticism

James's masterly summary of Fechner's general view in this regard. "The original sin, according to Fechner, of both our popular and our scientific thinking, is our inveterate habit of regarding the spiritual not as the rule but as an exception in the midst of nature. Instead of believing our life to be fed at the breasts of the greater life, our individuality to be sustained by the greater individuality, which must necessarily have more consciousness and more independence than all that it brings forth, we habitually treat whatever lies outside of our life as so much slag and ashes of life only ; or if we believe in a Divine Spirit, we fancy him on the one side as bodiless and nature as soulless on the other. What comfort or peace, Fechner asks, can come from such a doctrine ? The flowers wither at its breath, the stars turn into stone ; our own body grows unworthy of our spirit and sinks into a tenement for carnal senses only. The book of nature turns into a volume on mechanics, in which whatever has life is treated as a sort of anomaly ; a great chasm of separation yawns between us and all that is higher than ourselves, and God becomes a nest of thin abstractions."

It is sufficiently well known that primitive man did not indulge in these "thin" views of nature. He interpreted the events and changes around him on the analogy of human activities ; he looked upon them as manifestations of living wills. And indeed how could he do otherwise ? For as yet he knew of no mode of activity other

72

Animism, Ancient and Modern

than his own. At first those objects and happenings were singled out which were of most practical interest, or which most distinctly forced themselves upon the attention. The beast of prey which threatened his life, the noisy brook, the roaring waves, the whisperings and cracklings in the woods —all argued the presence of life and will. So too with mountains, avalanches, sun, moon, stars, clouds, caves, fire, light, dark, life, death. So more especially with the storm which sweeps across the land, the thunder which shakes the solid earth, and the lightning which flashes from the one side of heaven to the other. Such were the phenomena on which his intellect worked, and in which he discovered all manner of useful or harmful causal relations. Such were the phenomena which produced in him emotions of awe and terror, joy and delight. To all of them he ascribed mental life like unto his own. Indeed it was only by such a view that he could at all understand them, or bring himself into living connection with them.

From these primitive times onward, each century in the history of civilisation has brought a wider outlook. But the original tendency to animism has persisted and still persists. It has behind it an undying impulse. It manifests its vitality, not only among the uninstructed masses, but in the most select ranks of scientists and philosophers. And thus it is not too much to say that the idea of a universal life in nature is as firmly rooted to-day as it was in the dawn of

Nature Mysticism

man's intellectual development. The form in which the idea has been presented has changed with the ages. Mythology succeeded animism, and has in turn yielded to many curious and vanished theories, polytheistic, gnostic, pantheistic, and the rest. Now, the belief in distinct beings behind natural phenomena has virtually disappeared. Not so the belief in some form of universal life or consciousness—of which belief representative types will be given directly.

Of the persistence of the mental attitude in the modern child, Ruskin gives a charming example, in his " Ethics of the Dust." " One morning after Alice had gone, Dotty was very sad and restless when she got up ; and went about, looking into all the corners, as if she would find Alice in them, and at last she came to me, and said, ' Is Alie gone over the great sea ? ' And I said, ' Yes, she is gone over the great deep sea, but she will come back again some day.' Then Dotty looked round the room ; and I had just poured some water out into the basin ; and Dotty ran to it, and got up on a chair, and dashed her hand through the water, again and again ; and cried, ' Oh, deep, deep sea ! Send little Alice back to me.' " On this, Ruskin remarks—" The whole heart of Greek mythology is in that ; the idea of a personal being in the elemental power ; of its being moved by prayer ; and of its presence everywhere, making the broken diffusion of the element sacred." It would seem that Dotty did not definitely personify the

74

Animism, Ancient and Modern

element, but was rather in the animistic stage. The identifying of the natural element or object with a definite personality is a further step taken, as Ruskin says, by the Greeks pre-eminently. But the beauty and the suggestive quality of the incident remain, whichever view be taken.

A still more deeply suggestive example is found in Wordsworth's description of a boyish night adventure of his on Esthwaite Lake. For it shows the inner workings of a mind impressed by specially striking natural objects, and by the obscurely realised powers which they dimly manifest.

> " I dipped my oars into the silent lake,
> And as I rose upon the stroke my boat
> Went heaving through the waters like a swan ;—
> When, from behind that craggy steep till then
> The horizon's bound, a huge peak, black and huge,
> As if with voluntary power instinct
> Upreared its head.   I struck and struck again ;
> And, growing still in stature, the grim shape
> Towered up between me and the stars, and still,
> For so it seemed, with purpose of its own,
> And measured motion like a living thing,
> Strode after me.   With trembling oar I turned,
> And through the silent waters made my way
> Back to the covert of the willow-tree ;
> There in her mooring-place I left my bark,
> And through the meadows homeward went, in grave
> And serious mood.   But after I had seen
> That spectacle, for many days my brain
> Worked with a dim and undetermined sense
> Of unknown modes of being."

Nature Mysticism

There we have revealed to us the soul of animism whether ancient or modern !

The older animism was crude and uncritical. In proportion as men learnt to reflect upon their experience, it was bound to be modified, and to submit to reactionary influences. Such was the case at the very beginning of philosophical and scientific enquiry—and such was the case also at the opening of the " modern " era. Speaking generally, it may be said that as knowledge of natural law extended, the idea of mental activities in external nature was ousted. Mechanical views of the universe gradually prevailed, and reached a passing climax in Descartes' contention that even animals are automata !

" A passing climax "—for worse was to come. Man himself was to be brought under the remorseless sway of physics interpreted by mathematics. The *Homme Machine* idea found stalwart supporters, and gained many adherents. All forms of animism seemed to be overwhelmed once for all. The nature-mystic appeared to be an idle dreamer or a deluded simpleton. Nor is the course of such exaggerations yet ended. In the pages of the " Nineteenth Century," Huxley could seriously propound as a thesis for discussion the question— " Are animals automata ? " And books with such titles as " The Human Machine " have still considerable circulation.

But just as criticism undermined the immaturities and exaggerations of the older animism, so

76

Animism, Ancient and Modern

is it undermining the more dangerous arrogance of an exaggerated and soulless materialism. Speculation is now trending back to a critical animism, and, enriched by all that physical science has had to give, is opening out new world-views of transcendent interest. The nature-mystic is coming into his own again. It must be his care to keep abreast of thought and discovery, and so avoid that tendency to exaggeration, and even fanaticism, which has, in the past, so greatly damaged the cause of Mysticism at large.

The animistic theory is now being propounded thus. Why should not all transfers of energy, whether in living or non-living bodies, be accompanied by a " somewhat " that is akin to man's mental life ? The arguments in favour of such a view are numerous, many-sided, and cumulative. The hypothesis of evolution gives them keen edge and gathering force. Behind the cosmic process men feel there must be a creative power, an animating impulse. The struggle upwards must mean something. Mechanism is but a mode of working—its Ground is soul, or spirit.

Thus a new day is dawning for a soundly critical animism. It is realised that to formulate " laws " in accordance with which certain modes of happening take place is not to pierce to the heart of things, but to rest on the surface. Mechanism explains nothing and leaves us poor indeed ! Whereas, the universe is a majestic manifestation of Becoming—of a veritable development of life.

Nature Mysticism

The line between organic and inorganic is fading
more and more from the minds of investigators.
Protoplasm, for instance, mingles together mechanical, chemical, and vital in a fused whole, which it
passes the wit of man to analyse. The connection
between body and soul is similarly found to defy
the old distinctions between matter and mind.
Clearly a universal life is pulsating in the whole ;
genuine impulses, not mechanical stresses and
strains, are the causes of the upward sweep into
fuller consciousness and richer complexity of
experience. The old conception of a world soul
is achieving a new lease of life, and is dowering
science with the human interest and the mystic
glow it so sorely lacks.

CHAPTER XI

WILL AND CONSCIOUSNESS IN NATURE

THE idea that inorganic nature is not merely informed by reason, but is also possessed of will and consciousness, will strike many serious students as bizarre and fanciful. There is an enormous amount of initial prejudice still to be overcome before it can secure a fair general hearing. It will therefore be advisable to pass in review the teachings of certain modern thinkers, of recognised authority, who have espoused and openly advocated this bizarre idea. And with a view to insuring further confidence, the *ipsissima verba* of these authorities will be freely quoted, where there may be fear of misunderstanding or misrepresentation. The review will be confined to modern thinkers, because the views of the ancients in this regard, though frequently of intense interest, will not carry weight in a matter which so largely depends upon recent research and speculation.

Leibniz profoundly influenced the course of what we may term " animistic " thought by his doctrine of monads. Whereas Descartes had defined substance as extension, Leibniz conceived it as activity, or active force, and as divided up into an

Nature Mysticism

infinite number and variety of individual centres, each with its own force or life, and, up to a certain point, each with its own consciousness. All beings are thus essentially akin, but differ in the grades of consciousness to which they attain. But since consciousness depends on organisation, and since organisation is constantly developing, there is continuous progress. Each individual monad develops from within by virtue of a spiritual element which it possesses—that is to say, not mechanically, but from an internal principle, implying sensation and desire. These monads, when looked at from without, are grouped together into various extended objects. If we ask Leibniz how such inwardly developing centres are combined together into a universe, his reply is that God has so ordered things that each monad develops in definite relation to all the rest; they all keep time, like clocks with different works, springs, pendulums, but regulated to mark simultaneously each period of time as it passes. This is the famous theory of pre-established harmony.

This doctrine grants the nature-mystic all he needs, but in an artificial way which fails to carry conviction. The universe is split up into isolated units which have no real connection with each other save through ideas in the mind of God. Communion with nature, however, should be more direct and more organic than that effected by a pre-established harmony. Is it possible to retain the strong points of the theory while securing

80

Will and Consciousness in Nature

organic interpenetration of all modes of existence?
Lotze, for one, deemed it possible. Here is an
interesting and typical passage from his " Philosophy of Religion." " If it is once held conceivable
that a single supreme intelligence may exert an
influence on the reciprocal relations of the elements of the world, then similar intelligence may
also be imagined as immediately active in all these
individual elements themselves; and instead of
conceiving them as controlled merely by blindly
operative forces, they may be imagined as animated spiritual beings, who strive after certain
states, and offer resistance to certain other states.
In such case there may be imagined the gradual
origin of ever more perfect relations, from the
reciprocal action of these elements, almost like
the reciprocal action of a human society; and
that too without necessarily arriving at the assumption to which we are here inclined, of a single,
supreme, intelligent Being. Our reasoning issues
rather in a sort of polytheistic or pantheistic
conception, and that too in quite tolerable agree-
ment with experience."

Lotze, then, conceives the monads to be organically related, and so combined into one world.
He himself inclines to regard them as all dependent
upon one supreme Being. But it is to be carefully
observed that he does not negative the pluralist
hypothesis as inconceivable or impracticable. Indeed, a little later in the same context, he allows
that " a multiplicity of beings who share with each

other in the creation and control of the world " is
more in harmony with the immediate impressions
of experience than " the hasty assumption of one
only supreme wisdom, from which as their source
the imperfections of the world, that in fact
are manifest to us, are much more difficult to com-
prehend." Lotze may thus be summoned as a
supporter of the contention (urged in an earlier
chapter) that the Pluralist may be a genuine
mystic. Interpenetration and co-operation may
supply the place of the metaphysical unity at
which the Absolutists aim. But the main point
here is, that Lotze conceives the universe as
organically and spiritually related in all its parts.
It all shares in a common life.

Of a monadistic character, also, are the two
closely related views known as the Mind-Dust
theory, and the Mind-Stuff theory. The former
postulates particles or atoms of mind, distinct from
material atoms, but, like them, pervading all
nature, and, under certain conditions, combining
to form conscious mind. The latter does not thus
separate mind and matter, but assumes that
primordial units of mind-stuff sum themselves
together and engender higher and more complex
states of mind, and themselves constitute what
appears to us as matter. James in his larger
Psychology keenly criticised this " psychic
monadism," and has in his Oxford Lectures on
a " Pluralistic Universe," substantially modified
his criticism. It is not necessary to enter into

Will and Consciousness in Nature

further detail, but to grasp the fact that such modern scientists as Clifford inclined to see in the world, at every point, a manifestation of some grade of consciousness, and therefore of kinship. The noted French philosopher, Renouvier, has also resuscitated the monadistic theory in a form more closely allied to that of Leibniz.

Discussion of the merits and demerits of these various views is not now in question, but only their value as evidence of the trend towards a critical animism. The inadequacy of the mechanical view came home even to a mathematician like Clifford!

We turn to a very different form of speculation, yet one equally favourable to the essential contention of the nature-mystic—that of Schopenhauer, a philosopher whose system is attracting closer and keener attention as the years pass by. Certain of his views have been cursorily mentioned in what has preceded, and will find further mention in what is to follow. But here, the aim is to focus attention on his fundamental doctrine, that the Ground of all existence is Will. His line of argument in arriving at this conclusion is briefly to be stated thus. The nature of things-in-themselves would remain an eternal secret to us, were it not that we are able to approach it, not by knowledge of external phenomena, but by inner experience. Every knowing being is a part of nature, and it is in his own self-consciousness that a door stands open for him through which he can approach nature. That which makes itself most immediately known within himself is will ; and in this will is to be found the *Welt-stoff*. Let Schopenhauer speak for himself. " Whoever, I say, has with me gained this conviction . . . will recognise this will of which we are speaking, not only in those phenomenal existences which exactly resemble his own, in men and animals, as their inmost nature, but the course of reflection will lead him to recognise the force which germinates and vegetates in the plant, and indeed the force through which the crystal is formed, that by which the magnet turns to the North Pole, the force whose shock he experiences from the contact of two different kinds of metal, the force which appears in the elective affinities of matter as repulsion and attraction, decomposition and combination, and, lastly, even gravitation, which acts so powerfully throughout matter, draws the stone to the earth and the earth to the sun—all these, I say, he will recognise as different only in their phenomenal existence, but in their inner nature as identical, as that which is directly known to him so intimately and so much better than anything else, and which in its most distinct manifestation is called will."

Here again we have standing ground for the creed and the experiences of the nature-mystic. All forms and modes of existence are akin, and differ only in their phenomenal conditions. Whether Schopenhauer has not laid too exclusive an emphasis on will ; whether he has not unnecessarily chosen the lowest types of will as primitive

Will and Consciousness in Nature

—these are questions to be discussed elsewhere. Enough that we have in this theory a definite return to critical animism. He holds the universe to be throughout of the same " stuff," and that stuff is psychic or spiritual. Body and soul, matter and spirit, are but different aspects of the same underlying Reality.

Nevertheless, one question does press upon the nature-mystic. Is the will to be conscious of its activities ? Schopenhauer's Ground-will is a blindly heaving desire. If his contention be granted, Nature Mysticism will be shorn of its true glory. Communion with nature, though it rest on passive intuition, must somehow be associated with consciousness, if it is to be that which we best know. That is to say, nature's self-activity must be analogous to our own throughout—analogous, not identical. And such a conclusion commends itself to a thinker as careful and scientific as Stout, who in his " Manual of Psychology " writes as follows : " The individual consciousness, as we know it, must be regarded as a payment of a wider whole, by which its origin and its changes are determined. As the brain forms only a fragmentary portion of the total system of natural phenomena, so we must assume the stream of individual consciousness to be in like manner part of an immaterial system. We must further assume that this immaterial system in its totality is related to nervous processes taking place in the cortex of the brain."

Nature Mysticism

So, too, James, in his " Varieties of Religious Experience," declares that " our normal waking consciousness, rational consciousness as we call it, is but one special type of consciousness ; whilst all about it, parted from it by the filmiest of screens, there lie potential forms of consciousness entirely different. We may go through life without suspecting their existence ; but apply the requisite stimulus and at a touch they are there in all their completeness, definite types of mentality and adaptation. No account of the universe in its totality can be final which leaves these other forms of consciousness quite disregarded."

A thinker of a very different type, Royce, in his " World and the Individual," concurs in this idea of a wider, universal consciousness. " We have no right whatever to speak of really unconscious Nature, but only of uncommunicative Nature, or of Nature whose mental processes go on at such different time-rates from ours that we cannot adjust ourselves to a live appreciation of their inward fluency, although our consciousness does make us aware of their presence. . . . Nature is thus a vast conscious process, whose relation to time varies vastly, but whose general characteristics are throughout the same. From this point of view evolution would be a series of processes suggesting to us various degrees and types of conscious processes. The processes, in case of so-called inorganic matter are very remote

86

Will and Consciousness in Nature

from us, while in the case of the processes of our fellows we understand them better." Again he calls Nature " a vast realm of finite consciousness of which your own is at once a part and an example."

A thinker of still another type, Paulsen, whose influence in Germany was so marked, and whose death we so lately lamented, was whole-heartedly a sympathiser with Fechner's views. How James also sympathised with them we saw at the beginning of the last chapter. Paulsen, on his own account, writes thus : " Is there a higher, more comprehensive psychical life than that which we experience, just as there is a lower one ? Our body embraces the cells as elementary organisms. We assume that in the same way our psychical life embraces the inner life of the elementary forms, embracing in it their conscious and unconscious elements. Our body again is itself part of a higher unity, a member of the total life of our planet, and together with the latter, articulated with a more comprehensive cosmical system, and ultimately articulated with the All. Is our psychical life also articulated with a higher unity, a more comprehensive system of consciousness ? Are the separate heavenly bodies, to start with, bearers of a unified inner life ? Are the stars, is the earth an animated being ? The poets speak of the earth-spirit ; is that more than a poetic metaphor ? The Greek philosophers, among them Plato and Aristotle, speak of astral spirits ; is

Nature Mysticism

that more than the last reflection of a dream of childish fancy ? "

And thus we have come to the fullness of the nature-mystic's position. Reason, will, feeling, consciousness, below us and above us. As Nägeli, the famous botanist puts it, " the human mind is nothing but the highest development on our earth of the mental processes which universally animate and move nature." To this world-view the child of nature and the philosopher return again and again. Deep calls unto deep. The exaggerated and dehumanising claims of purely physical and mechanical concepts may for a time obscure the intuition by their specious clarity, but the feelings and the wider consciousness in man reassert themselves. The stars of heaven no longer swing as masses of mere physical atoms in a dead universe, they shine in their own right as members in a living whole. Wordsworth speaks for the forms of life beneath us when he exclaims :

> " And 'tis my faith that every flower
> Enjoys the air it breathes."

Emerson speaks for the realm of the inorganic when he assures that :

> " The sun himself shines heartily
> And shares the joy he brings."

The great world around us is felt to pulse with inner life and meaning. It is seen, not only as real, not only as informed with reason, but as sentient. The old speculations of Empedocles that

Will and Consciousness in Nature

love and hate are the motive forces in all things
gleams out in a new light. And that sense of oneness with his physical environment which the
nature-mystic so often experiences and enjoys is
recognised as an inevitable outcome of the facts
of existence. Goethe is right :

> " Ihr folget falsche Spur ;
> Denkt nicht, wir scherzen !
> Ist nicht der Kern der Natur
> Menschen im Herzen."

CHAPTER XII

MYTHOLOGY

THE materials are now fairly complete for understanding the rise and development of animism. The untrained primitive intellect was stirred by vague intuitions—stimulated by contact with an external world constituted of essentially the same " stuff " as itself—and struggled to find concrete expression for its experiences. The root idea round which all else grouped itself was that of the agency of indwelling powers like unto man's, but endowed with wider activities, and unhampered by many human limitations. The forms of expression adopted often appear to us to be almost gratuitously absurd ; but when we put ourselves as nearly as may be at the primitive point of view, we realise that they were not even illogical. The marvel is that out of the seething chaos of sensations and emotions there could arise the solid structure of even the simplest kinds of conceptual, ordered knowledge.

There are few critics, however, who are not now prepared to put themselves into sympathetic touch with the primitive thinker ; but there are still many who hesitate, or refuse, to allow any

Mythology

value to the products of his thinking. These products are too frequently dismissed as the fancies and babblings of ages in which real knowledge was not as yet a practicable achievement. Such an estimate is as unfair as it is unphilosophical. It disregards the part played by intuition, and it is blind to the germs of truth which were destined to ripen into noble fruit. Mother Earth, with air and sunshine, and starry heaven above, nurtured men's thoughts and souls as well as their bodies.

There is more than an analogy between the childhood of the race and the childhood of the individual. And just as the child plunges us at times, by questions, into problems of the deepest import, so is it with unexpected flashes of insight preserved for us in the records, written or unwritten, of the earliest workings of the human mind. "The soul of man" (says Caird), "even at its worst, is a wonderful instrument for the world to play on ; and in the vicissitudes of life, it cannot avoid having its highest chords at times touched, and an occasional note of perfect music drawn from it, as by a wandering hand on the strings."

It is remarkable how, in spite of the enormous advances made by civilised thought, our concepts and hypotheses, not excepting those deemed most fundamental, are being constantly modified. How much more would change prevail in ages when structured knowledge had hardly come into

Nature Mysticism

existence. But whether the pace of change be slow or rapid, the same impelling cause is at work—man's determination to find fuller expression for his intuitional experience. Animism developed into mythology, mythology into gnomic philosophy, and this again became differentiated into science, art, philosophy, and theology. In the earlier stages, the instability of men's imaginings and conceptions was kaleidoscopic; but it was no more governed by wanton fickleness and caprice than is the course of modern thought. The human spirit was striving then, as now, to realise worlds vaguely experienced and dimly surmised. The more imperfect expression was continuously yielding place to the less imperfect—the lower concept continuously yielding place to the higher. And at the base of the whole great movement upwards was sensation, as the simplest mode of intuition—sensation being, in its various forms and developments, the outcome of man's intercourse with an external world that, in its essence, is spiritual like himself.

The main error of animism was its failure to draw distinctions. It tended to look upon nature as equally and fully human in all its parts. It translated its intuitions of kinship into terms of undifferentiated similarity, and thereby entangled itself in hopeless confusions. But by degrees the stubborn facts of existence made their impression, and compelled men to realise that life on the

Mythology

human plane is one thing, and quite another on the plane of external nature. The attempt to absorb the larger truth thus sighted was only partially successful, and gave birth to the wondrous world of mythology. Its chief characteristic was that the will which was at first conceived to be within, or identical with, the object, was separated from the object and accorded a personal, or quasi-personal existence. In other words, the non-human character of external nature was acknowledged, while at the same time the human type of will was preserved. The river, for example, was at first regarded as itself an animated being ; then the will it manifests was separated from the material phenomena, and by personification became a river-god who rules the phenomena. So the sun gave rise to the conception of Apollo ; and, by a double remove, the lightning became a weapon in the hand of Zeus. There was thus added to man's world of things a second world of spiritual beings who animated and swayed the things. The change was momentous ; but it held fast to the original root idea of nature as a manifestation of spiritual powers.

It was inevitable that the mythological system should collapse when once the spontaneous play of imaginative thought gave place to self-conscious, systematising reflection. The mass of incoherent, and often contradictory myths, in which the true was so strangely blended with the false, the beautiful with the ugly or revolting, fell almost by its own weight. The more solid materials it contained were first transmuted into allegories, and then expressed in the language of science and philosophy. The original intuitions, which had been encumbered with degrading superstitions and deadening ceremonies, again declared their power and their persistence, though sometimes under disguises which rendered them hard to recognise.

And very instructive and arresting it is to note how haltingly conscious reflection assimilated the rich store of ideas which spontaneous intuition had seized upon whole ages previously. For instance, Anaxagoras taught that since the world presents itself as an ordered and purposeful whole, the forming force or agency must also be purposeful. Following up this line of thought, and guided by the analogy of human activities, he declared this agency to be Nous, or reason—or, better still, "reason-stuff." This conclusion was rightly deemed to be of profound importance. And yet, when we analyse it, it seems at first sight difficult to see wherein consists its originality. For what else but this had been taught by the age-old animism that had preceded it ? And yet all who were fitted to judge hailed the teaching as something radically new. It stirred far-reaching currents in the deep ocean of Greek philosophic thought ! How can we explain the apparent anomaly ? The fact is we have here a typical instance of the transition from intuition to reflective thought.

Mythology

There is a conscious grasp of promptings dimly felt—a grasp that rendered possible the advance from mythology to science and philosophy. The gain was enormous, and bore abundant fruit; but it should not be allowed to obscure the merit, nor the value, of the primitive intuition on which it was based.

It must be evident that similar examples might be multiplied indefinitely, and certain of them will be adduced when typical nature-myths are under more detailed consideration. It is because of these germ truths enshrined in the ancient myths that so many bygone modes of thought and expression last on into the new order. Ruskin, in genuine mythological style, often used the term "gods," and explains his meaning thus: "By gods, in the plural, I mean the totality of spiritual powers delegated by the Lord of the universe to do in their several heights, or offices, parts of His will respecting man, or the world that man is imprisoned in; not as myself knowing, or in security believing, that there are such, but in meekness accepting the testimony and belief of all ages ... myself knowing for indisputable fact, that no true happiness exists, nor is any good work ever done by human creatures, but in the sense or imagination of such presences."

The nature-mystic need not be ashamed of mythology. Sympathetically studied, it affords abundant proof of the working of intuition and mystic insight. It enabled multitudes of men,

95

Nature Mysticism

long before science and philosophy became conscious aims, to enter into some of the deepest truths of existence, and to live as members of a vast spiritual hierarchy embracing earth and heaven.

CHAPTER XIII

POETRY AND NATURE MYSTICISM

WHAT a charm the nature deities of Greece and
Rome can still exercise! How large the place
they still occupy in poetry, art, and general
culture! At times some of our moderns are
tempted to look back with a very real measure of
regret to the golden age of mythology, feeling that
in comparison the present is often sadly dull and
sordid. Wordsworth's great sonnet gives classical
expression to this mood, and rises to a white heat
of indignation :

> " Great God ! I'd rather be
> A Pagan suckled in a creed outworn,—
> So might I, standing on this pleasant lea,
>   Have glimpses that would make me less forlorn ;
> Have sight of Proteus rising from the sea ;
>   Or hear old Triton blow his wreathèd horn."

It may be said that the poet is carried away by
the feeling of the moment. It finds expression,
however, more calmly, though no less decidedly,
in a less well-known passage :

> " O fancy, what an age was that for song !
>   That age, when not by laws inanimate,
>   As men believed, the waters were impelled,
>   The air controlled, the stars their courses held ;

H 97

Nature Mysticism

> " But element and orb on *acts* did wait
> Of Powers endued with visible form instinct,
> With will, and to their work by passion linked."

Clearly mythology and nature-poetry are closely allied though centuries come between : they breathe the same air though " creeds outworn " have yielded place to deeper faiths. And we are driven to ask—Is poetry in its turn to go ?—poetry, at any rate, of the old, simple, direct sort ? Reflective reason is asserting itself : critical methods play havoc with the spontaneous creations of imagination. Coleridge, in one of his moods, would almost persuade us so. In his " Piccolomini " Max is conversing with the Countess :

> " The intelligible forms of ancient poets,
> The fair humanities of old religion,
> The power, the beauty and the majesty,
> That had their haunts in dale, or piny mountain,
> Or forest by slow stream, or pebbly spring,
> Or chasms and wat'ry depths ; all these have vanished ;
> They live no longer in the faith of reason."

And yet Coleridge did not allow that the outlook was wholly sad. His young soldier continues :

> " But still the heart doth need a language, still
> Doth the old instinct bring back the old names."
>   . . . and even at this day
> 'Tis Jupiter who brings whate'er is great,
> And Venus who brings everything that's fair."

No, poetry is not dead, and never will die. Certain stages in human progress may favour its

98

Poetry and Nature Mysticism

spontaneity more than others—critical reflection may cloud over the naïve and fresh directness of experience—but behind each natural phenomenon is the immanent idea, the phase of cosmic will and consciousness, which science, and logic and critical analysis can never exhaust. The intuition has its rights as well as the syllogism, and will always ultimately assert them. Whereas science reduces the world to mechanism, poetry intuits and struggles to express its inner life ; and since this inner life is inexhaustible, poetry is immortal. Emerson seized upon this truth with characteristic keenness of perception allied with feeling.

> " For Nature beats in perfect time
>   And rounds with rhyme her every rune,
>   Whether she work in land or sea,
>   Or hide underground her alchemy.
>   Thou canst not wave thy staff in air ,
>   Or dip thy paddle in the lake,
>   But it carves the bow of beauty there,
>   And the ripples in rhymes the oar forsake.
>   The wood is wiser far than thou ;
>   The wood and the wave each other know
>   Not unrelated, unaffected,
>   But to each thought and thing allied
>   Is perfect Nature's every part,
>   Rooted in the mighty heart."

And again in his " Ode to Beauty," he rejoices in the

> " Olympian bards who sung
>   Divine Ideas below,
>   Which always find us young
>   And always keep us so."

99

Nature Mysticism

Thank Heaven, we have not yet come to think that the highest form of wisdom is enshrined in the *sesquipedalia monstra* of chemical formulæ, still less in the extreme abstractions of mathematics. Not that such formulæ have not a beauty, and even a Mysticism of their own; their harmfulness comes from the exclusiveness of their claims when they are advanced as an adequate description (sometimes explanation !) of existence at large and of life in particular. The biological formulæ, based on mathematics, at which Le Dantec, for instance, has arrived, if taken at their author's valuation, and if consistently applied, would make the sublimest poetry to be greater folly than the babble of a child. The nature-mystic may, or may not, allow them a relative value according as he considers them to be valid or invalid abstractions from observed facts; but he knows that the most valid of them are exceedingly limited in their scope and superficial in their bearing: and it remains a standing wonder to him that any trained intellect can fail to realise their miserable inadequacy, in view of the full rich current of living experience.

One of the chief merits of genuine nature-poetry is that it keeps us in close and constant touch with sense experience, and at the same time brings home nature's inner life and meaning. It is not a mere string of metaphors and symbols based on accidental associations of ideas, but an expression and interpretation of definite sensa-

Poetry and Nature Mysticism

tions and intuitions which result from the action of man's physical environment upon his deepest and most delicate faculties. "High art" (says Myers) "is based upon unprovable intuitions; and of all arts it is poetry whose intuitions take the brightest glow, and best illumine the mystery without us from the mystery within."

But more especially, poetry is essentially ani-mistic. It produces its characteristic effect by creating in the mind the sensuous images which best stimulate the mind to grasp the immanent idea, and it presents those images as instinct with life and movement—sometimes it goes so far as to personify them. This is what Matthew Arnold meant when he declared poetry to be "simple, sensuous, passionate." Coleridge has a good illustration (quoted by Nisbet). He observes that the lines:

> " Behold yon row of pines that shorn and bowed
>   Bend from the sea-blast, seen at twilight eve "—

contain little or no poetry if rearranged as a sentence in a book of topography or description of a tour. But the same image, he says, rises into the semblance of poetry if thus conveyed:

> " Yon row of black and visionary pines
>   By twilight glimpse discerned! Mark how they flee
>   From the fierce sea-blast, all their tresses wild
>   Streaming before them."

The difference in the two presentations consists

in this, that in the second of them there is a suggestion of life and movement which is lacking in the first. But why the different effect upon the mind? Nisbet answers—" the visual and motor centres contribute to the creation of the image "— an answer admirably typical of the fashionable psychology of the day, not necessarily wrong in itself, but so curiously incomplete! Nisbet holds that man himself is a machine, and thus could not easily go farther—especially as his own machinery evidently would not work any farther. The nature-mystic begins at the other end. He holds that even the inorganic world is more than machinery—that it is instinct with life and meaning. When, therefore, life and movement are attributed to seemingly inert or motionless objects, there is a responsive thrill caused by the subconscious play of primitive intuitions that are based on the facts of existence. Spirit realises more vividly than in normal experience that it is in touch with spirit.

Contrast with the psychological dictum the proud claim advanced by Emerson.

> " The gods talk in the breath of the woods,
>   They talk in the shaken pine,
>   And fill the reach of the old sea-shore
>   With melody divine.
>   And the poet who overhears
>   Some random word they say
>   Is the fated man of men,
>   Whom the ages must obey."

Poetry and Nature Mysticism

There are two claims presented here—one directly, the other indirectly. The direct claim is that there are seers and interpreters who can catch the mystic words that nature utters. The indirect is that the general mass of humanity have the capacity for sharing the experiences of their poet leaders. The one class are endowed to an exceptional degree with receptivity; the other are also receptive, but are dependent on those who can give expression to the intuitions which are, though in varying degrees, a possession common to humanity at large. As Sir Lewis Morris puts it :

> " All men are poets if they might but tell
> The dim ineffable changes which the sight
> Of natural beauty works on them."

He, too, recognises the mediating function of the poet.

> " We are dumb,
> Save that from finer souls at times may rise
> Once in an age, faint inarticulate sounds,
> Low halting tones of wonder, such as come
> From children looking on the stars, but still
> With power to open to the listening ear
> The Fair Divine Unknown, and to unseal
> Heaven's inner gates before us evermore."

And what is this but to claim for the mass of men, in varying but definite degrees, a capacity for the experiences of the nature-mystic ? Poetry and Nature Mysticism are linked together in an im-

103

perishable life so long as man is man and the world is the world.

It will have been apparent that in what has been said about the relation of poetry to science, there has been no shadow of hostility to science as such, but only to the exclusive claims so often preferred on its behalf. Let a French philosopher of the day conclude this chapter by a striking statement of the relationship that should exist between these seemingly incompatible modes of mental activity. In a recent number of the " Revue Philosophique," Joussain writes as follows :

" On peut ainsi se demander si le savant, à mesure qu'il tend vers une connaissance plus complète du réel, n'adopte pas, en un certain sens, le point de vue propre au poète. Boileau disait de la physique de Descartes qu'elle avait coupé la gorge à la poésie. La raison en est qu'elle s'en tenait au pur mécanisme et ne definissait la matière que par l'étendue et le mouvement. Mais la physique de Descartes n'a pu subsister. Et, avec la gravitation universelle que Leibniz considérait à juste titre, du point de vue cartésien, comme une *qualité occulte*, avec les attractions, les répulsions, les affinités chimiques, avec la théorie de l'évolution, la science tend de plus en plus à pénétrer la vie réele des choses. Elle se rapproche, bon gré, mal gré, de la metaphysique et de la poésie, en prenant une conscience plus profonde de la force et du devenir. C'est qu'au fond la pensée humaine est une, quelle que soit la

Poetry and Nature Mysticism

diversité des objets auxquels elle s'applique, art,
science, poésie, métaphysique, répondant, chacun
à sa façon au même désir, chacun reflétant dans la
conscience humaine les multiples aspects de la vie
innombrable."

CHAPTER XIV

THE BEAUTIFUL AND THE UGLY

A CHARGE frequently brought against the nature-mystic is that he ignores the dark side of nature, and shuts his eyes to the ugly and repulsive features of the world of external phenomena. If nature can influence man's spiritual development, what (it is asked) can be the effect of its forbidding and revolting aspects ? Is the champion of cosmic emotion and of Nature Mysticism prepared to find a place for the ugly in his general scheme ? The issue is grave and should not be shirked. It is, moreover, of long standing, having been gripped in its essentials by many thinkers of the old world, more especially by Plato, Aristotle, and Plotinus.

Let us begin by examining one or two characteristic statements of the indictment that there are ugly, and even revolting, objects in a world we would fain think fair. Jefferies says of certain creatures captured in the sea : " They have no shape, form, grace, or purpose ; they call up a vague sense of chaos which the mind revolts from. . . . They are not inimical of intent towards man, not even the shark ; but there the shark is, and

106

The Beautiful and the Ugly

that is enough. These miserably hideous things of the sea are not anti-human in the sense of persecution, they are outside, they are ultra and beyond. It is like looking into chaos, and it is vivid because these creatures, interred alive a hundred fathoms deep, are seldom seen ; so that the mind sees them as if only that moment they had come into existence. Use has not habituated it to them, so that their anti-human character is at once apparent, and stares at us with glassy eye."

Kingsley, in his " At Last," asks, " Who will call the Puff Adder of the Cape, or the Fer-de-lance, anything but horrible and ugly ; not only for the hostility signified, to us at least, by a flat triangular head and heavy jaw, but by the look of malevolence and craft signified, to us at least, by the eye and lip ? "

Frederic Harrison puts the case from the more general point of view : " The world is not all radiant and harmonious ; it is often savage and chaotic. In thought we can see only the bright, but in hard fact we are brought face to face with the dark side. Waste, ruin, conflict, rot, are about us everywhere. . . . We need as little think this earth all beauty as think it all horror. It is made up of loveliness and ghastliness ; of harmony and chaos ; of agony, joy, life, death. The nature-worshippers are blind and deaf to the waste and the shrieks which meet the seeker after truth. . . . The poets indeed are the true authors of the beauty and order of nature ; for they see it

by the eye of genius. And they alone see it.
Coldly, literally examined, beauty and horror,
order and disorder seem to wage an equal and
eternal war."

In considering the substance of these strong
statements, characteristic of very different types
of mind, we note in the first place that two different
problems are to some extent fused—that of the
ugly, and that of the morally evil. Of course, it
is frequently impossible to separate them ; still,
for purposes of analysis, the attempt should be
made ; especially as our present quest is æsthetic
rather than ethical.

In the second place it must be remembered
that the nature-mystic is by no means a nature-
worshipper. His claim of kinship with nature
surely implies the contrary ! He knows that evil
and ugliness (however interpreted) are in man, and
he expects therefore to find them permeating the
whole.

Confining our attention as far as may be to the
æsthetic aspect of the objections raised, let us at
once define and face the real issue now before us,
namely, the significance for the nature-mystic of
what is called " ugliness."

There are certain judgments known as æsthetic
—so called because they determine the æsthetic
qualities of objects. And it is agreed, with practical unanimity, that they rest much more upon
feeling and intuition than upon discursive reason.
To this extent they rank as genuine " mystical "

The Beautiful and the Ugly

modes of experience, and from this point of view have bulked largely in the systems of mystics like Plato and Plotinus. But while claiming them as mystical, it is necessary to note that they possess a characteristic which constitutes them a special class. They imply reference to a standard, or an ideal. The reference need not be made, indeed seldom is made, with any conscious apprehension of the standard; but the reference is none the less there, and a judgment results. The place of reflective reasoning process which characterises the logical judgment is filled by a peculiar thrill which accompanies a feeling of congruence or incongruence, according as the ideal is satisfied or otherwise.

It is in accord with this view of the æsthetic judgment that while, for reason, the outward form and semblance of the object is of subsidiary import, save from the point of view of abstract form and physical quality, for the æsthetic feeling or intuition it is paramount. For example, a botanist, *quâ* botanist, will reck little of beauty of colour, or curve, or scent—indeed at times his interest in a plant may be in inverse ratio to its beauty. But the lover of flowers, or the poet, or the artist, will fix upon such æsthetic qualities as determining his mood and judgment. Not that the reflective and the æsthetic judgments are antagonistic—they are supplementary, and, when rightly appreciated, they are interdependent; nevertheless, they must not be confused.

109

Nature Mysticism

'The doctrine of Plotinus, the prince of mystics, is very helpful when the problem of the ugly is in debate, and fits in admirably with the considerations just advanced. His theory was that material objects are beautiful in proportion as they share in reason and form. The converse of this proposition is, that objects are ugly in proportion as they lack the capacity for sharing in reason and form. Passing over certain other phases of his doctrine, let us see how far this theory will carry us in answering the question—Is there in nature such a thing as ugliness, in any absolute sense of the term ?

Matter, as known to the modern scientist, is universally possessed of form of some kind, and is, moreover, found to share in reason, when tested by its responsiveness, so to speak, to the processes of human ratiocination—or, in other words, by its obedience to natural law. It would seem to follow that there is no object in nature which is absolutely ugly. And the conclusion surely commends itself to common sense. If, in spite of this, certain objects are called " ugly," what is intended? Following up the lead of Plotinus, we seem to be driven to the conception of " degrees of beauty " —of " higher " and " lower " forms of beauty. And the moment the existence of such " degrees " is accepted, the æsthetic horizon is indefinitely extended. The whole problem assumes larger and more generous proportions, especially when viewed in the light of the evolution hypothesis.

The Beautiful and the Ugly

For where there are degrees, or stages, it is an easy step to conceive of transition from stage to stage. An ugly object is only relatively ugly; and by entering into new relations with its environment may be raised to even higher rank in the æsthetic scale of values. In brief, true progress becomes possible for the whole universe. Herbert Spencer stopped short at progress from the homogeneous to the heterogeneous. It is more interesting, not to say, inspiring, to postulate increase of capacity for sharing in reason and form. The vast process of evolution may then be viewed as an upward sweep into fuller beauty and into correspondingly fuller life.

Of the fact that there is such an upward process, there is abundant and accumulating evidence. The struggle upwards of organic life, culminating so far, in man as we know him—the increasingly complex beauty of natural forms—the haste of nature to conceal her scars—all alike speak of a striving upward. Nay, we are being told that the atoms themselves, so long regarded as ultimates, have been subjected to the evolutionary stress and strain, and have advanced from the simplest forms to higher and more complex symmetries. And in another field, the arts, more particularly painting and the drama, almost demand the recognition of some such principle of progress; for they are constantly and necessarily using elements which in themselves are accounted ugly, for the production of their supremest beauties.

111

Nature Mysticism

The use of discords in music is singularly suggestive in this regard. There are combinations of musical sounds which, when produced as isolated combinations, are harsh, and even painful. But let them be heralded by other chords, and let them be parted from by suitable resolutions, and they can charm, or thrill, or kindle deep emotion. What does this fact imply? That discords in music, when used with knowledge and mastery, do not take their places as aliens in musical progressions—as insertions of ugliness in a texture of surrounding beauty—*but as themselves beautiful.* Their æsthetic value is gained by their being linked up in a network of relations which makes them part and parcel of that which is an ordered and rational whole. In short, discords are potential beauties; they have capacity for form and reason.

The ugly, then, is not to be opposed to the beautiful as its contrary, but as standing in the relation to it of the less to the more perfect. There will thus be grades of beauty as there are grades of reality. And mystic intuition will have corresponding grades of dignity and insight. The grand process of evolution is thus revealed as a many-sided whole—the amount of real existence increases in proportion to the increase of capacity for sharing in form and reason; and along with this goes a growth in power to appreciate the ever higher forms of beauty which emerge in the upward-striving universe.

112

The Beautiful and the Ugly

A further thought calls for emphasis. For beings like ourselves, living under conditions which involve so many limitations, a *purely* æsthetic judgment is practically out of our reach. And on this score also we may venture to tone down the strong expressions used by Jefferies in his estimate of the anti- or ultra-human character of the strange creatures in the sea. Individual likings and dislikings are the resultants of an enormously complex system of impulses, instincts, prejudices, motives, habits, associations, and the rest. Few of these factors appear above the threshold of consciousness, though they are continually and influentially operative. Hence it by no means follows that because a particular object is displeasing or disgusting to one individual, or group of individuals, it will be so to all. So undoubted is the resulting relativity of our æsthetic judgments that Hegel was inclined to hold that below the level of man and art there is no real ugliness at all. "Creatures" (he says) "seem ugly to us whose forms are typical of qualities opposed to vitality in general, or to what we have learnt to regard as their own special or typical form of animate existence. Thus the sloth as wanting in vitality, and the platypus as seeming to combine irreconcilable types, and crocodiles and many kinds of insects, simply, it would appear, because we are not accustomed to consider their forms as adequate expressions of life, are all ugly."

Nature Mysticism

Just as, in music, discords become beautiful by being brought into fitting relations with other parts of an ordered whole, so is it with objects which are usually considered ugly, but which are capable of æsthetic beauty when treated in pictures by masters of their craft. To set them in new and fitting relations of light and shade, of colour and composition, is to transform them. Schopenhauer lays great stress on the transforming power of art. He instances many typical paintings of the Dutch school, simple interiors, homely scenes, fruit, vegetables, the commonest tools and utensils, even dead flesh—all are taken up into material for pictures, and, in their special setting, compel our admiration.

We have in these facts concerning pictorial art, a strong corroboration of the inference from the use of discords in music—the relativity of ugliness, and the possibility of its progressive transformation. But there is a further point to be emphasised, one which music, by reason of its abstractness, could not well enforce, and one which is of profound significance for the nature-mystic. Pictorial art is concerned with the representation of external objects. How explain its transforming power ? Schopenhauer has an excellent answer to the question. He says that the artist is endowed with an exceptional measure of intuitive insight. He enjoys a genuine vision of the Idea immanent in the object he reproduces in his particular medium—he fixes attention upon this Idea,

114

The Beautiful and the Ugly

isolates it, and reveals much that would otherwise escape notice. The result is that his skill enables others to slip into his mood and share his insight.

It is on some such lines as those tentatively traced in the last few paragraphs that the most hopeful solution of the problem of the ugly must be sought. The heart of the matter is that there is no object in external nature which is absolutely ugly—no object which cannot, even as things are, be transformed to some degree by being set in fitting relation to others—no object which is not capable of progress in its capacity for sharing and manifesting the form and reason towards which the universe is striving. Should there be thinkers who, like Kingsley, cannot quite rid themselves of the feeling that ugliness is an absolute reality—a positive mode of existence over against beauty—they can only take refuge in the wider problem of evil. But care must be exercised, as before observed, to distinguish between moral evil and physical ugliness. To what extent the one may be reflected in the other is a question on which it would not be safe to dogmatise. The main theory, however, stands out clearly, and involves a belief that the material phenomena of the universe, as a grand whole, enjoy a wholesome freedom from positive ugliness. Tennyson's " Ancient Sage " expresses the nature-mystic's hopes concerning the fundamental beauty of the world he loves.

115

Nature Mysticism

" My son, the world is dark with griefs and graves,
So dark, that men cry out against the Heavens,
Who knows but that the darkness is in man ?
The doors of Night may be the gates of Light ;
For wert thou born or blind or deaf, and then
Suddenly healed, how wouldst thou glory in all
The splendours and the voices of the world !
And we, the poor earth's dying race, and yet
No phantoms, watching from a phantom shore,
Await the last and largest sense to make
The phantom walls of this illusion fade,
And show us that the world is wholly fair."

CHAPTER XV

NATURE MYSTICISM AND THE RACE

THE fundamental postulates and principles of a
consistent Nature Mysticism have now been expounded with a fullness sufficient to allow of a
soberly enthusiastic study of the detail of our
subject. Let it be noted, however, that though
a detailed application of general conclusions is
henceforth to be the main business, there will be
no forsaking of the broadly human standpoint.
For it has been shown, more especially in the
chapter on poetry, that the nature-mystic does
not arrogate to himself any unique place among
his fellows, nor seek to enjoy, in esoteric isolation,
modes of experience denied to the mass of humanity.
Wordsworth, for instance, though a prince among
modern mystics, appealed with confidence to his
countrymen at large : his " we " was in constant
evidence—and an ever-growing multitude of nature-
lovers responds to his appeal. That is to say, the
faculty of intuition he demands is to be found, in
varying degrees, latent at least, if not evolved, in
the normal human being. The gifted seer seizes
and interprets what his less gifted brother obscurely
feels. Can we trace this mystic power of nature

Nature Mysticism

on the scale of history at large? If the power is real, it should be possible to recognise its grander workings. Moreover, a wide outlook will help us to avoid exaggerations, preciosities, and fanaticisms.

Here, then, is our starting-point for detailed study. If it be true that all normal members of the race share in varying degrees the faculty of mystic intuition, then nature must have had a moulding effect not only on certain gifted individuals, but on the character and destiny of whole communities, peoples, and empires. As behind the language of the Greeks there were age-long promptings of subconscious metaphysics, so behind the æsthetic and spiritual development of this remarkable people there must have been age-long promptings of subconscious mystical intuitions stimulated by the influences of natural phenomena. The moulding force of the immanent ideas, and of the inner life of things, is, for the race at large, and for certain peoples in particular, continuous, cumulative, massive. True, it takes effect chiefly in the sphere of the subconscious. But he will be a poor student of history who fails to reckon with those subtler forces which, though obscure in their action, often extend so widely and go so deep.

An eloquent evidence of nature's power to mould is to be found in the contrasted characteristics of the great religions. The hardy peoples of north-western Europe were nurtured under stormy

118

Nature Mysticism and the Race

skies, were girt in by stern, avalanche-swept mountains, and struggled strenuously against the hardships of rigorous and lengthy winters. What wonder that they filled their heaven with *Sturm und Drang*—with titanic conflicts of the gods—and heard it echoing with the whirl of hunting, the riot of feasting, and the clang of battle? Their religion was strenuous as their lives—free and fierce—yet tinged with a melancholy that promised rich developments.

The favoured Greeks of classical times, "ever delicately walking on most pellucid air," or rocked on the isle-strown waters of the sapphire Ægæan, expanded their soul-life in an environment teeming with light and colour, with harmony and form. For them, therefore, Apollo bent his burnished bow and launched his myriad shafts of gold; Aphrodite embodied visions of foam-born beauty; Athene stood forth in panoply of reason and restraint. Nature herself lured them to evolve ideals of law and order, of disciplined thought and perfectly proportioned art. What wonder that, prompted by mystic impulses and visions, they purged their inherited religion of its grosser features, and made it a vehicle for philosophic thought and spiritual aspiration.

Pass to the wandering children of the desert, cradled amid the great silences of space and time, swallowed up of vastness. Above them by day the burning vault of blue, by night the wheeling galaxies—around them the trackless levels of a

119

Nature Mysticism

thirsty land. Such influences sank deep into their souls, and imparted depth and intensity to their views of the source and meaning of that vastness. Nor can we wonder that in such an environment, the premonitions of the spiritual unity of existence, that were stirring in many hearts, found special sustenance.

Let it be clearly understood that in the striking and unmistakable illustrations just adduced, there is no mere question of the influences of physical environment on social organisation or economic development—though these also react in a thousand ways upon ideas and ideals—but a question of moulding spiritual concepts by the direct influence of the ideas and impulses manifested in external nature. Man's soul was in constant, if generally subconscious, communion with his material environment, and his thinking was thereby largely coloured and fashioned. And if the kind and quality of the influence vary from age to age, and from people to people, it is not the less continuously potent. The complexities of modern life, the interminglings of civilisations, tend to obscure its manifestations; science, wrongly pursued, seems hostile to continued vigour. But underneath the play of the cross-currents on the surface, is the resistless swing of the tide.

An illustration of another class is found in Max Müller's brilliant lectures on " Physical Religion," the chief theme of which is the development of Agni, the Vedic god of fire. The starting-point

Nature Mysticism and the Race

was the sensuous perception of the physical qualities of fire. The Idea and the will immanent in these qualities gradually raised men's thoughts from the material to the spiritual, until the Eastern world attained to what Max Müller calls " a precious line from the Veda "—" He who above the gods was the One God "—composed at least one thousand years before the Christian era. It was not the result of a supernatural revelation, but a natural outcome of man's thoughts guided and moulded by impressions of outward phenomena. That is to say, as Max Müller observes, there was nothing in it artificial—simply that which man could not help saying, being what he was and seeing what he saw.

In the instances just advanced, the broad principle is most assuredly established that nature has a definite and continuous effect upon the development of man's conduct and thought. And as a consequence of this, we may affirm that Wordsworth's experience is true, in its measure, of all normal members of the race who are in touch with nature :

> " Therefore am I still
> A lover of the meadows and the woods
> And mountains ; and of all that we behold
> Of this green earth ; both what they half create
> And what perceive ; well pleased to recognise
> In nature and the language of the sense,
> The anchor of my purest thoughts, the nurse,
> The guide, the guardian of my heart, and soul
> Of all my moral being."

121

Nature Mysticism

Why, even old Dr. Johnson in his Dictionary days would write to his friend Langton, in Lincolnshire: " I shall delight to hear the ocean roar, or see the stars twinkle, in the company of men to whom Nature does not spread her volumes or utter her voice in vain." And let us observe, that the naturalness of his feeling keeps him to the simplest, almost monosyllabic, English !

CHAPTER XVI

THALES

In an earlier chapter mention was made of that truly remarkable group of thinkers who, in the sixth century before the Christian era, made the momentous transition from mythology and tradition to philosophy and science. It was also pointed out that these pioneers, bold as they were, could not shake themselves free from the social and intellectual conditions of their day. And it is precisely this fact of what may be termed contemporary limitations that makes a review of their speculations so valuable to a student of Nature Mysticism. For they lived in times when the old spontaneous nature beliefs were yielding to reflective criticism. Their philosophising took its spring from the fittest products of the mythopœic faculty, and thus remained in living contact with the primitive past, while reaching forward, in the spirit of the future, to an ordered knowledge of an ordered whole. The chief object of their search was the *Welt-stoff*—the substance of the universe—and they were guided in their search by the dominating concepts which had emerged in the long course of the animistic and

123

Nature Mysticism

mythological stages. Certain forms of external existence have impressed themselves upon the general mind, notably those of water, air, and fire; and to these the reflecting mind naturally turned in its earliest efforts to discover the Ground of things. The interest taken by the nature-mystic in this group of thinkers is twofold. Firstly, he finds that in their speculations there is a large element of primitive intuition, embodied in concepts fashioned by the spontaneous play of reflective thought and free imagination. Closeness to nature is thus secured. And secondly, he rejoices in the fact that these speculations, crude and premature as they inevitably were, contained germs of thought and flashes of insight which anticipate the most advanced speculative science and philosophy of the present day. He maintains that here is corroboration of his view of intuition. Nature was the teacher—and it was to intuition that she chiefly addressed herself; and the intellect—keen and fresh, but untrained—was able to seize upon the material presented, and to fix it in concepts and theories which share in nature's universal and unending life.

Water, air, and fire—what an enormous number and variety of natural phenomena range themselves under these heads! If we try to understand why they were singled out in turn, in the search for the *Welt-stoff*, we shall have penetrated far into the Nature Mysticism of these famous " elements."

124

Thales

Starting, then, with Thales, we ask why he fixed upon water in his attempt (the earliest recorded) to determine the constitution of the universe? What were the properties, qualities, and functions of that " element " which arrested his attention, and governed his crude, but acute and original, speculations? As already remarked, existing cosmological conceptions played an important rôle, more especially that of the great primeval ocean on which the world was supposed to float. This cosmographical ocean and its accompanying myths will be considered in a subsequent chapter. But restricting our view at present to the physical aspects of water, it is not wholly impossible to recover, and sympathise with, his train of reasoning.

Water is wonderfully mobile, incessantly changing, impelled apparently by some inherent principle of movement. Its volatility, also, is very marked; it passes from solid to liquid, and liquid to vapour, and easily reverses the series. More especially would the old-world thinker be struck by the phenomena of the circulation of water. He would see the vapour drawn up by the sun from lake and ocean, seeming to feed the heavenly fires, and returning to earth in the form of rain. He concluded that this must represent the flow of the cosmic process as a whole. Again, in the falling of dew, in the gatherings of mists, and in the welling-up of fountains, the solid materials of the world are apparently passing into a liquid state.

Nature Mysticism

Thales was not the first to note these things. They had been subtly modifying the thoughts of men for untold generations. But he was the first whom we know to have gathered together into a definite theory the vague intuitions which had been so long unconsciously operative. He singled out this mobile element and saw in it the substance of the flux of the world as a whole.

His theory of movement took a wide range. He did not separate the thing moved from the moving force; nor did he draw any distinction between the organic and inorganic—the mechanical and the vital. He regarded all modes of motion as essentially spontaneous and self-determined. Moreover (as Aristotle tells us) he identified this inherent principle of change with what is divine in nature and in the soul. That is to say, the Real, for Thales, is living impulse and continuous process. It is experienced in man's conscious activities, and constitutes the principle of unity in every mode and form of existence.

It is on the organic side of this speculation that Aristotle, probably biased by his biological studies, chiefly dwells. Is it possible to trace the grounds of which Thales based his wider induction? Aristotle helps us. He supposes his predecessor to have noted that water and life seem to be inseparable, and that moisture is necessary to the germination and development of all known organisms. It was natural to conclude that the principle of life is in the water—the conclusion of the reason

Thales

also harmonising with the intuition stimulated by movement. Nor was the inference altogether unwarranted. Put into historical perspective, it still retains its force and value. The latest biological authorities tell us that all branches of the zoological family tree were formed on the moist shores of large water basins, and that there is no form of life, not only terrestrial, but even of the deep seas which has not passed through a littoral phase. In other words, it is still allowable to hold that the " moist," as Thales generally called his primal element, contains one of the secrets of life. So close is the earliest to the latest pronouncement on the origin of life on the globe !

Reviewing this brief exposition of the leading doctrine of an ancient speculation, what bearing has it on the principles of Nature Mysticism as laid down in preceding chapters ? Certain fairly obvious ones. Thales was guided by impressions received from the qualities, behaviour, and functions of water ; and they led him to attribute a plastic life to matter. It would be modernising him too severely to style him a hylozoist. But his ascription of a soul to the magnet and to amber carries him far on the way to that metaphysical world-view. Deeply suggestive also is the saying which, if not rightly attributed to him, is at least characteristic of his school—" All things are full of the gods." We may therefore infer that the physical properties of water are such as to suggest the ideas which have culminated in modern

Nature Mysticism

animism. That is to say, water is capable of producing intellectual and spiritual, as well as what are termed physical effects. The deeper view of intuition is justified. And Thales, by virtue of the whole trend and outcome of his speculations, may claim an honoured place in the ranks of the nature-mystics.

CHAPTER XVII

THE WATERS UNDER THE EARTH

WE have found that the constant movement and change manifested in the circulation of the waters of the globe impressed the mind of Thales and largely determined the course of his speculation. When his great successor, Heracleitus, passed from water to fire, in his search for the *Welt-stoff*, he by no means became insensible to the mystic appeal of running water. " All things are flowing." Such was the ancient expression of the universal flux ; and it is plainly based on the analogy of a stream. If Heracleitus was not its author, at any rate it became his favourite simile. " We cannot step" (he said) "into the same river twice, for fresh and ever fresh waters are constantly pouring into it." And yet, in a sense, though the waters change, the river remains. Hence the statement assumed a form more paradoxical and mystical—" We step into the same river, and we do not step into it ; we are, and we are not."

Moving water, then, has the power of stimulating emotion and prompting intuition ; and this power is manifested in exceptional degree when the source from which the water issues, and the goal

K   129

Nature Mysticism

to which it flows, are unknown. These conditions are best satisfied in the case of streams that flow in volume through subterranean caverns. The darkness contributes its element of undefined dread, and the hollow rumblings make the darkness to be felt. What more calculated to fill the mind of the child of nature with a sense of life and will behind the phenomena ? The weird reverberations are interpreted by him as significant utterances of mighty, unseen powers, and the caves and chasms are invested with the awe due to entrances into the gloomy regions where reign the monarchs of the dead.

True, it may be said, for the child of nature. But are such experiences possible for the modern mind ? Yes, if we can pierce through the varied disguises which the intuitional material assumes as times and manners change. Coleridge, for instance, is thrown into a deep sleep by an anodyne. His imagination takes wings to itself ; images rise up before him, and, without conscious effort, find verbal equivalents. The enduring substance of the vision is embodied in the fragment, " Kubla Khan," the glamour of which depends chiefly on the mystical appeal of subterranean waters. We are transported to where

> " Alph, the sacred river, ran
> Through caverns measureless to man,
> Down to a sunless sea."

These three lines make a deeper impression than any others in the poem, and form its main theme.

The Waters Under the Earth

Nor is the feeling of the supernatural unrecognised. Spirits are near with prophetic promptings. From a deep chasm the sacred river throws up a mighty fountain, and for a short space wanders through wood and dale, only to plunge again into its measureless caverns, and sink in tumult to a lifeless ocean :

> "And mid this tumult Kubla heard from far
> Ancestral voices prophesying war."

Thus when Coleridge's imagination was set free, the mode of feeling declared itself which had persisted down the ages to the present. The primitive experience is there in its essentials, enriched by the æsthetic and intellectual gains of the intervening centuries. Doubtless there is a living idea, or rather a group of living ideas, behind the phenomena of subterranean waters.

Wordsworth has described a more personal experience which chimes in with all that has been said.

> "Through a rift
> Not distant from the shore on which we stood,
> A fixed, abysmal, gloomy, breathing place—
> Mounted the roar of waters, torrents, streams
> Innumerable, roaring with one voice !
> Heard over earth and sea, and, in that hour,
> For so it seemed, felt by the starry heavens."

If the modern poet could be thus affected, how much more the primitive man who looked down on water falling into chasms, or rushing through their depths. It was natural that such experiences should find expression in his systems of mythology.

131

Nature Mysticism

The general form they assume is that of springs and rivers in the underworld, the best known of which appear in the Græco-Roman conceptions of Hades. Homer makes Circe direct Odysseus thus. He is to beach his ship by deep-eddying Oceanus, in the gloomy Cimmerian land. "But go thyself to the dank house of Hades. Thereby into Acheron flow Pyriphlegethon and Cocytus, a branch of the water of the Styx, and there is a rock and the meeting of the two roaring waters."

Such were the materials which, with many additions and modifications, developed into the Hades of Virgil's sixth Æneid, with its lakes, and swamps and dismal streams. The subterranean waters figured also in the Greek mysteries, and are elaborated with much detail in Plato's great Phædo Myth—in all these cases with increasing fullness of mystical meaning. In the popular mind they were incrusted with layers of incongruous notions and crude superstitions. But, as Plato, for one, so clearly saw, there is always at their core a group of intuitions which have their bearing on the deepest problems of human life, and are capable of moulding spiritual concepts.

Still more obviously suffused with mystic meaning and influence are the Teutonic myths concerning the waters of the underworld. The central notion is that of Yggdrasil, the tree of the universe—the tree of time and life. Its boughs stretched up into heaven; its topmost branch overshadowed Walhalla, the hall of the heroes.

The Waters Under the Earth

Its three roots reach down into the dark regions beneath the earth; they pierce through three subterranean fountains, and hold together the universal structure in their mighty clasp. These three roots stretch in a line from north to south. The northernmost overarches the Hvergelmer fountain with its ice-cold waters. The middle one overarches Mimur's well with its stores of creative force. The southernmost overarches Urd's well with its warmer flow. They are gnawed down below by the dragon Nidhögg and innumerable worms; but water from the fountain of Urd keeps the world-ash ever green.

Hvergelmer is the mother fountain of all the rivers of the world—below, on the surface of the earth, and in the heaven above. From this vast reservoir issue all the waters, and thither they return. On their outward journey they are sucked up and lifted aloft by the northern root of the world tree, and there blend into the sap which supplies the tree with its imperishable strength and life. Rising through the trunk, they spread out into the branches and evaporate from its crown. In the upper region, thus attained, is a huge reservoir, the thunder-cloud, which receives the liquid and pours it forth again in two diverse streams. The one is the stream of fire-mist, the lightning, which with its " terror-gleam " flows as a barrier round Asgard, the home of the gods; the other falls in fructifying shower upon the earth, to return to its original source in the under-

133

Nature Mysticism

world. The famous maelström is the storm-
centre, so to speak, of the down-tending flood.
The fountain Hvergelmer may therefore be regarded as embodying impressions made on the
Teuton mind by the physical forces of the universe
in the grand activities of their eternal circulation.
But their source was hidden.

The southernmost well has the warmer water of
the sunny climes—the fountain of Urd. The
Norns, the three sisters who made known the
decrees of fate, come out of the unknown distance,
enveloped in a dark veil, to the world tree, and
sprinkle it daily with water from this fountain,
that its foliage may be ever green and vigorous.
Urd is the eldest of the three, and gazes thought-
fully into the past ; Werdandi gazes at the present;
and Skuld gazes into the future. For out of the
past and present is the future born. The fountain of Urd may be regarded as the embodiment
of impressions of a spiritual force which upholds
and renews the universe.

Mimur, the king of the lower world, is the
warder of the central fountain, and round its
waters are ranged his golden halls. The fountain
itself is seven times overlaid with gold, and above
it the holy tree spreads its sheltering branches.
It is the source of the precious liquid, the mead,
which belongs to Mimur alone, and rises from an
unknown depth to water the central root. In its
purity, it gives the gods their wisdom and power.
But the mead which rises in the sap is not entirely

The Waters Under the Earth

pure ; it is mixed with the liquids from the other fountains. Thus earth is not like heaven. Nevertheless, though thus diluted, it is a fructifying blessing to whomsoever may obtain it. Around it grow delightful beds of reeds and bulrushes ; and bordering it are the Glittering Fields, in which grow flowers that never fade and harvests that are never reaped ; in which grow also the seeds of poetry. In short, Mimur's well is the source of inspiration and creative power.

These Teutonic notions of the waters under the earth have been dwelt upon somewhat fully, partly because they are not so well known as the classical myths—partly because they present such a decided contrast to the classical myths—but mainly because of their wealth of mystic suggestiveness. Let it not be thought that they form a group of elaborate symbols—were that the case their interest for the natural mystic would be vastly decreased. They are almost wholly the spontaneous product of the mythopœic faculty ; they were genuinely believed as presentations of realities. They are primitive intuitions embodied to form a primitive philosophy of life. They glow with mystic insight. Under the forms of subterranean fountains that well forth life, physical, æsthetic, spiritual, is mirrored the life of the universe, which wells from unknown depths, and returns to the deeps from which it emanated. And inasmuch as these ideas were largely suggested by the circulation of the waters of the

135

Nature Mysticism

globe, the Teutonic child of nature joins hands with the nature-philosopher Thales. The Reality is ultimately the same for both; the substance of the universe is living movement.

Yet another type of the mystic influence of subterranean watercourses will serve to illustrate the deepening processes to which all concrete forms, derived from intuitions, must be subjected. Near to Banias in Northern Palestine, at the base of an extensive cup-shaped mound, afar from human habitations, is one of the two chief sources of the Jordan. The rushing waters pour out of the ground in sufficient volume to form at once a river. The roar and tumult are strikingly impressive. Peters, on whose description of the place I have largely drawn, presumes that this was the site of an ancient temple of Dan. The worship at this temple was of the primitive sort, " such as was befitting the worship of the God who exhibited himself in such nature forces." We are therefore carried back to the mythological stage, for which the gushing forth, in volume, of subterranean waters was a manifestation of the life in, or behind, the natural phenomenon, and roused a peculiar kind of emotion.

We are carried on to a much more advanced stage when we come to the feelings represented in the 42nd Psalm. Peters argues that this Psalm, which so vividly describes the roaring of the waters was, " in its original form, a liturgical hymn sung at the great autumnal festival by

The Waters Under the Earth

worshippers at this shrine, where served, according to tradition, the descendants of Moses." On this supposition how pregnant with historical import become the well-known words : " One deep calleth another because of the noise of the water-pipes ; all thy waves and billows are gone over me." It is no mere analogy or symbol that is here employed (though such elements may be mingled in the complex whole) but an intuition yearning to express itself that life's burden would be lightened if the secret of the gushing waters could be read.

And it is thus that we arrive at the fundamental intuition common to the various modes of experience just reviewed. The subterranean waters spring from an unknown source, or fall into an unknown abyss. In both cases there is a sense of having reached the limits of the knowable, combined with a sense of inexhaustible power. The beyond is vague and insubstantial, but it is instinct with life and purpose. Man's spirit may shrink before the unknown—but he fills the empty regions with forms and objects which rob them of much of their strangeness and aloofness, and bring them within the range of his hopes and fears. There, as here (he feels), there must be interpenetration of spirit by spirit.

CHAPTER XVIII

SPRINGS AND WELLS

MILTON, in his noble "Ode on the Nativity," sings that, with the advent of the Saviour,

> "From haunted spring and dale,
>   Edged with poplars pale,
>   The parting genius is with sighing sent."

Is this a statement of fact? Largely so, if the reference is to the river gods, the Naïads, and water sprites, of classical mythology. But not true if the vaguer belief in spirits who preside over mossy wells and bubbling springs be taken into account, or if the faith in the healing or other virtues of the waters that issue from them be included in the underlying idea. No, not even in the most Christian countries of to-day is such faith extinct. One has but to remember the famous well at Auray, or the sacred fountain in the crypt of the church at St. Melars, to which whole crowds of pilgrims still resort, to realise how far this is from being the case. Scotland herself, for all her centuries of Puritanism, has not wiped her slate quite clean; still less the countries like Ireland and Brittany, which are so retentive of

138

Springs and Wells

the past. Nay, the present age is not content with its liberal supply of sacred springs, it must be adding new ones of its own! Let Lourdes be witness. And who shall say how many more are yet to come?

Very remarkable, both as illustrating Milton's Ode, and also the persistency of this particular form of superstition, is the story of the only real spring close to Jerusalem—Enrogel. It is identified by high authorities with the Dragon's Well, mentioned in a romantic passage of the book of the patriot, Nehemiah. Assuming the validity of this identification, we have a glimpse of times far earlier than the Hebrew occupation of the land. Primitive peoples often associated serpents with springs and wells, as incarnations of the spirit of the waters. A link is thus supplied which carries back the history to the animistic and mythological periods, in this case, prehistoric.

Retracing our course, we arrive at the time of the Hebrew occupation of the country. A purer form of religion has rejected most of the mythological material. But the old name of the spring remains, and, what is still more pertinent, the old belief in its healing power. We have evidence of this belief in St. John's Gospel, which contains the peculiar story of the healing at the pool of Bethesda, most probably connected with this same spring. The popular view that at times an angel came to trouble the water is perhaps an attempted explanation of its intermittent action.

Now should have come the time, according to

Nature Mysticism

Milton, for the departure of the sighing genius—
the dying out of the superstition. But those who
anticipate such a *dénoucment* will be grievously
disappointed. For the Jews still bathe in its
waters, at the times of overflow, for cure of various
maladies. And on the Christian side of the history,
it has gained the name of the Virgin's Pool!

Similar stories might be found in any part of
the globe where tradition is sufficiently continuous
to preserve them, testifying to the almost astounding persistency of belief in the power of
springing water. No doubt simple faith healing
has played its part—but that part is very subsidiary; the strongest influence has been that
exercised by the movement of the water itself,
suggesting as it does the idea of spontaneous life.
Not less surprising is the hold such springs retain
upon the imagination and affections. Pathetic
proof of this meets the traveller at every turn on
the west coast of Ireland. As he tramps the
byways and unfrequented paths of County Clare,
his eye is caught from time to time by an artless
array of shelves on the sloping banks of some
meadow spring. On the shelves are scanty votive
offerings, piteous to see. Piteous, not on the score
of the superstition which prompts them—that is
a matter to be dealt with in a spirit of broad
sympathy, on its historic and social merits—but
because of the dire poverty they reveal. Even
bits of broken crockery are held worthy of a
place at these little shrines; so bereft are the

140

Springs and Wells

peasantry of the simplest accompaniments of civilised life.

How thoroughly natural is the growth of such sentiments and beliefs! Jefferies felt the charm. "There was a secluded spring" (he writes) "to which I sometimes went to drink the pure water, lifting it in the hollow of my hand. Drinking the lucid water, clear as light itself in solution, I absorbed the beauty and the purity of it. I drank the thought of the element; I desired soul-nature pure and limpid."

Nor has the charm ceased to be potent for the new man in the new world. Walt Whitman knew it. Here is a delightful paragraph from his notes of " Specimen Days " : " So, still sauntering on, to the spring under the willows—musical and soft as clinking glasses—pouring a sizeable stream, thick as my neck, pure and clear, out from its vent where the bank arches over like a great brown shaggy eyebrow or mouth roof—gurgling, gurgling ceaselessly—meaning, saying something of course (if one could only translate it)—always gurgling there, the whole year through—never going out— oceans of mint, blackberries in summer—choice of light and shade—just the place for my July sun-baths and water-baths too—but mainly the inimitable soft sound-gurgles of it, as I sit there hot afternoons. How they and all grow into me, day after day—everything in keeping—the wild, just palpable, perfume, and the dapple of leaf-shadows, and all the natural-medicinal, elemental-moral influences of the spot."

141

Nature Mysticism

If these two passages be taken together, there will be few elements of mystic influence left un-noted. And how deeply significant the fact that each author instinctively and spontaneously associates with the limpid flow of the water the ideas of life and health! Were the old mythologists so very far from the truth? Is it so very hard to understand why wells and springs have had their thousands of years of trust and affection? Was it mere caprice that led our Teutonic fathers to place under the roots of the world-tree the three wells of force and life and inspiration?

A fine example of a more definitely mystic use of the ideas prompted by the sight of springing water, is found in Dante's "Earthly Paradise"—an example the more interesting because of its retention of what may be called the "nature-elements" in the experience.

> " The water, thou behold'st, springs not from vein,
>   Restored by vapour, that the cold converts ;
>   As stream that intermittently repairs
>   And spends his pulse of life ; but issues forth
>   From fountain, solid, undecaying, sure :
>   And, by the will omnific, full supply
>   Feeds whatsoe'er on either side it pours ;
>   On this, devolved with power to take away
>   Remembrance of offence ; on that, to bring
>   Remembrance back of every good deed done.
>   From whence its name of Lethe on this part ;
>   On the other, Eunoe : both of which must first
>   Be tasted, ere it work ; the last exceeding
>   All flavours else."

142

Springs and Wells

This passage, say the authorities, is linked on to the old Proserpine mystery, and is parallel to the Teutonic conceptions described in the last chapter.

Of quite exceptional character, yet best treated in the present connection, are the " wells " of eastern lands. Where the sources of springing water are rare and far distant from one another, the supply of water has to be supplemented by that from artificial pits, sunk with hard toil, often into the solid rock, and valued accordingly. Such " wells," in the stricter sense, are too directly associated with human labour in historic times, to allow much mythical material to accumulate around them. Still, from the simple fact of their dispensing water in arid and thirsty lands, they possess not unfrequently a rich store of family and tribal legends. And further, by reason of their very freedom from the cruder superstitions, the intuitions they prompted were from the first transparent and spiritual. Under such conditions the water is literally " life." And as the conception of life deepened, so did intuition become more delicate.

We have the early freshness of the feeling stimulated in an ancient strain, delightful in its naïve spontaneity.

> " Then sang Israel this song :
>   Spring up, O well, sing ye unto it :
> The well which the princes digged,
> Which the nobles of the people delved,
>   With the sceptre and with their staves."

143

Nature Mysticism

The deepening of the feeling came rapidly, and took exquisite form in the prophet's assurance that his people should "draw water out of the wells of salvation." But here mysticism was beginning to blend with symbolism, and the later developments of the idea pass over almost wholly into the sphere of reflective analogy.

So far as the nature-mystic is concerned, he emphasises the continuity of the feeling, from the earliest ages to the present, that in the phenomena of water gushing from a source we have a manifestation of self-activity, as immanent Idea and concrete will. And convinced of the validity of his contention, he is not surprised, as some may be, at the influence which wells and springs have wielded, and still do wield, over the human soul.

CHAPTER XIX

BROOKS AND STREAMS

THERE is a striking passage in Tylor's " Primitive Culture " which will admirably serve as an introduction to this chapter and the one which is to follow, on " Rivers and Waterfalls." " In those moments of the civilised man's life when he casts off hard dull science, and returns to childhood's fancy, the world-old book of nature is open to him anew. Then the well-worn thoughts come back fresh to him, of the stream's life that is so like his own ; once more he can see the rill leap down the hill-side like a child, to wander playing among the flowers ; or can follow it as, grown to a river, it rushes through a mountain gorge, henceforth in sluggish strength to carry heavy burdens across the plain. In all that the water does, the poet's fancy can discern its personality of life. It gives fish to the fisher, and crops to the husbandman ; it swells in fury and lays waste the land ; it grips the bather with chill and cramp, and holds with inexorable grasp its drowning victim. . . . What ethnography has to teach of that great element of the religion of mankind, the worship of well and lake, brook and river, is simply this—

Nature Mysticism

that what is poetry to us was philosophy to early man ; that to his mind water acted not by laws of force, but by life and will ; that the water-spirits of primeval mythology are as souls which cause the water's rush and rest, its kindness and its cruelty ; that lastly man finds, in the beings with such power to work him weal or woe, deities with a wider influence over his life, deities to be feared and loved, to be prayed to and praised and propitiated with sacrificial gifts."

Tylor has here given a masterly résumé of a large group of facts, and has viewed them from a particular angle—not quite that of the nature-mystic, though not so far removed as might appear. He does not make it appear that there was any organic connection between the phenomena and the mythology, nor even between the phenomena and the feelings which the modern man, in certain moods, feels stirring within him at their prompting. These myths are simply " fancies " ; the " feelings " are simply those of " the poet." The wider view adopted by so many philosophers and scientists (as was shown in the chapter on animism) does not seem to have won his adherence—perchance was not known to him. And yet in sentence after sentence he hovers on the brink of genuine Nature Mysticism. His sympathy with the leaping rill and the rushing river is deep and spontaneous ; he is evidently well pleased to open afresh " the world-old book of nature," and to read it in the light of " child-

Brooks and Streams

hood's fancy." The nature-mystic avers that what he deemed a recurrence of meaningless, if pleasant, " well-worn thoughts " was really an approach to the heart of nature from which an imperfect understanding of the place and function of science had carried him away. Not that the old forms should be perpetuated, but that the childlike insight should be cherished.

Water in movement in brooks and streams! Have we discovered the secret of it when we tell of liquids in unstable equilibrium which follow lines of least resistance ? It is a valuable advance to have gained such abstract terms and laws, so long as we remember they *are* abstractions. But it is a deadly thing to rest in them. How infinitely wiser is Walt Whitman, in his address to a brook he loved, than the man who coldly analyses, with learned formulæ to help him, and sees and feels nothing beyond. " Babble on, O brook " (Walt Whitman cries), " with that utterance of thine ! . . . Spin and wind thy way—I with thee a little while at any rate. As I haunt thee so often, season by season, thou knowest, reckest not me (yet why be so certain—who can tell ?)—but I will learn from thee, and dwell on thee—receive, copy, print, from thee."

Is this to indulge in vague anthropomorphic fancies—though not of the cruder sort, still of subjective value only ? The persistence, the vividness, and the frequency of such " imaginings " prove that the subjective explanation does not

147

Nature Mysticism

tell the whole tale. How natural, in the simplest
sense of the word, is Coleridge :

> " A noise like of a hidden brook
>   In the leafy month of June,
>   That to the sleeping woods all night
>   Singeth a quiet tune."

How earnest is Wordsworth as he opens out
glimpses of unknown modes of being in his address
to the Brook :

> "If wish were mine some type of thee to view
>   Thee, and not thee thyself, I would not do
>   Like Grecian artists, give the human cheeks
>   Channels for tears ; no Naiad shouldst thou be,—
>   Have neither limbs, feet, feathers, joints, nor hairs ;
>   It seems the Eternal Soul is clothed in thee
>   With purer robes than those of flesh and blood,
>   And hath bestowed on thee a safer good ;
>   Unwearied joy, and life without its care."

Again, what natural feeling declares itself in the
delightful Spanish poem translated by Longfellow :

> "Laugh of the mountain ! lyre of bird and tree !
>   Pomp of the meadow ! mirror of the morn !
>   The soul of April, unto whom are born
>   The rose and jessamine, leaps wild in thee !"

How deep, once more, the note sounded by Brown
in his lines on " The Well " :

> " I am a spring—
>   Why square me with a kerb ?
>
>   .   .   .   .   .
>
>   O cruel force,
>   That gives me not a chance
>   To fill my natural course ;

148

Brooks and Streams

With mathematic rod
Economising God ;
Calling me to pre-ordered circumstance
Nor suffering me to dance
Over the pleasant gravel,
With music solacing my travel—
With music, and the baby buds that toss
In light, with roots and sippets of the moss ! "

The longing for freedom to expand the dimly
realised and mystic elements in his soul-life was
stirred within him by the joyous bubbling of a
spring. To kerb the artless, natural flow is to
" economise God "—so the limitations and re-
strictions of the life that now is artificialise and
deaden the divine within us. There is more than
metaphor in such a comparison ; there is the
linkage of the immanent idea. His emotion
culminates in the concluding lines :

" One faith remains—
That through what ducts soe'er,
What metamorphic strains,
What chymic filt'rings, I shall pass
To where, O God, Thou lov'st to mass
Thy rains upon the crags, and dim the sphere.
So, when night's heart with keenest silence thrills,
Take me, and weep me on the desolate hills."

There are indeed but few with any feeling for
nature who have not been moved to special trains
of thought, the outcome of characteristic moods,
by the babblings and wayward wanderings of
brooks and rivulets. The appeal, therefore, is to a
wide experience. Can we be satisfied to join with

149

Nature Mysticism

Tylor in his sense of disillusionment ?   Or shall we strive to get yet nearer to the heart of things ? If we cling to the deeper view, to us, as to the men of old, the running stream will sing of the soul in nature.

CHAPTER XX

RIVERS AND LIFE

A RIVER is but a larger brook. And yet by virtue of its volume, it manifests features which are peculiarly its own, and exerts influences which have not alone affected individual moods and imaginings, but often profoundly modified and moulded the destinies of peoples and civilisations. The two outstanding instances are the Nile and the Ganges.

The Nile has attracted to itself, from the dawn of history to the present day, a peculiar share of wonder and renown. It is the longest river of its continent—possibly of the world; and the exploration of its sources is only just completed. It flows through a limestone country over which, save for its beneficent action, would drive the parched sands of the Libyan desert. Its periodic inundations, with their rich deposits of alluvial soil, repel the encroaching wastes, and solve the problem of the food supply. Egypt has with good reason been called " the gift of the Nile."

This river therefore possesses in a marked degree all the mystic influences of moving water, and emphasises them by physical and historical features

Nature Mysticism

of exceptional import. What wonder that it has had so direct a bearing on the spiritual development of the people on its banks, and that it entered into the very texture of their lives! It was, for the Egyptian, pre-eminently the sacred river—deemed to be one of the primitive essences—ranked with those highest deities who were not visible objects of adoration. As a form of God "he cannot (says an ancient hymnist) be figured in stone; he is not to be seen in the sculptured images upon which men place the united crowns of the North and the South, furnished with uraei." The honour thus conferred was but commensurate with the blessings he brought. For in what would have been a valley of death he was the sole source and sustainer of life. A further quotation from the beautiful hymn just mentioned will indicate the affection and mystic emotion he inspired. "Homage to thee, O Hapi! (i.e. the Nile). Thou comest forth in this land, and dost come in peace to make Egypt to live, O thou hidden one, thou guide of the darkness whensoever it is thy pleasure to be its guide. Thou waterest the fields which Ra hath created, thou makest all animals to live, thou makest the land to drink without ceasing; thou descendest the path of heaven, thou art the friend of meat and drink, thou art the giver of the grain, and thou makest every place of work to flourish, O Ptah! . . . If thou wert to be overcome in heaven the gods would fall down headlong, and mankind would perish."

Rivers and Life

In this passage the mystic observes how the natural power of running water to suggest spontaneous movement, and therefore life, is accentuated and defined by the actual results of the river's beneficent overflow. And a further step is taken when Hapi is addressed by the names of Ptah (as above) and Khnemu ; for he is not thus confused with the gods so named, but being the great life-supplier for the land, he is, like them, regarded as a creative power. The development of the ideas suggested is thus essentially parallel to that described in the chapter on the Teutonic myths of the three subterranean wells and the World-tree.

But can any distinctive features of the Egyptian religion be traced to the influences exerted by the phenomena of the Nile ? Most decidedly so— in two directions more especially. That religion is one of contrasts; it represents the world as a scene of titanic conflict. The realm of Osiris is opposed to that of Typhon—creation to destruction. And the master influence in shaping the form in which these contrasts were conceived was undoubtedly the Nile. On one side barren rocks and parched sands, and on the other the fertilising powers of the sacred stream. All around, vast solitudes, and along the river the hum of teeming communities and the rich fullness of prosperous civilisations. The world was visibly, for the Egyptian, a fierce recurring battle between life and death.

153

Nature Mysticism

And springing out of this appears the second great influence to be attributed to the famous river. The Egyptian grasped firmly and developed fully the doctrine of immortality. Doubtless many factors contributed to the peculiar form which his belief assumed, but none would be of more importance than the ever renewed gift of life which the Nile brought from an unknown and an unseen world. Hence also the connection between the Nile-god and Osiris, the god of the resurrection. So deeply were the world-views and spiritual experiences of the Egyptians influenced by the mystic's powers of the Nile—by the immanent ideas therein made concrete. The Egyptians, in their turn, influenced the Hebrews, the Greeks, and the Romans; and these, again, have influenced the race. Who shall estimate the effect on the human mind of the physical phenomena of this single river!

When we turn to the story of the Ganges, a further mystical concept comes into view—that of purification. It is manifestly suggested by the cleansing qualities of water, and has exercised an important function in the development of certain moral ideas and ideals. Bathing in running water to cleanse the stains of the body led on to, and combined with, the concept of cleansing the stains of the soul. But even thus the dominant suggestion of life declares itself, as is specially obvious in the case of Christian baptism, where the washing with water symbolises not only the

Rivers and Life

cleansing of the soul, but the new birth, the higher life of the spirit. It is by keeping in mind these blended concepts that we shall best understand the story of the Ganges.

All the larger rivers of India are looked upon as abodes and vehicles of the divine essence, and therefore as possessed of power to cleanse from moral guilt. Their banks, from source to sea, are holy ground, and pilgrims plod their way along them to win merit—a merit that is measured by the years of travel and the sanctity of the stream. Of all the great rivers in this ancient land, the Ganges is the noblest. Mother Gangâ stands supreme. No water such as hers for washing away the stains of the most heinous crimes. She has bands of priests who call themselves her "Sons," and who conduct pilgrims down the flights of steps that line her banks, aid them in their ablutions, and declare them clean. To die and to be buried near the stream is in itself sufficient to win an entrance to the realms of bliss. "Those who, even at a distance of a hundred leagues, cry Gangâ, Gangâ, atone for the sins committed during three previous lives." In short, the hold the river has obtained upon the affections and imaginations of the Hindus is marvellously firm and lasting.

Of course a river so renowned has its wreath of myths and legends, characterised, in this instance, by the prodigality of the Eastern mind. It is not necessary to linger over these, save in so far as to

155

Nature Mysticism

note that they ascribe a divine origin to the sacred stream; the sense of power and movement issuing from the world of the unseen is no less strong than that aroused by the Nile; though it finds strangely different modes of expression, its essential character is the same. Interesting and typical is the Hindu belief that the spot where flow together the waters of the Ganges, the Jumna and the Sarasvati is one of the most hallowed in a land of holy places. "These three sacred rivers form a kind of Tri-murti, or triad, often personified as goddesses, and called ' Mothers.' " With such facts in view, it would be hard to exaggerate the influence of rivers on the development of the Hindu's speculation and practice, and more especially of his mysticism.

Such intuitions and beliefs find their full flower in the conception of the river of life—the stream, pure as crystal, that, with exulting movement onward, brings to men the thrill of hope and the inspiration of progress to a world beyond. It pulses and swings in the glorious sunshine—it reflects the blue of heaven—it sweeps superbly with unsullied current past every obstacle, and bursts through every barrier:

at ille
Labitur et labetur in omne volubilis aevum.

Yes, the Nile, the Ganges, the Rhine, the Thames, and a thousand other rivers of renown have had, and still have, their part to play in the cosmic drama and in the development of man's spiritual

Rivers and Life

nature. Generation after generation has found them to be capable of stirring peculiar emotions, and of stimulating profound thoughts on the mystery of life. And all these powers are concentrated and sublimated in this glorious vision of "the river of water of life that flows from the throne of God."

CHAPTER XXI

RIVERS AND DEATH

THE world of fact, no less than the world of abstract thought, is full of contradictions and unsolved antinomies. Here is one such contradiction or antinomy. Moving water, it has been shown, is suggestive of life. But over against it we find a suggestion of death. Indeed there has been a widely diffused belief in a river of death—a striking foil to the inspiring mysticism of the river of life. The old-world mythology taught, in varying forms, but with underlying unity of concept, that there is a river, or gulf, which must be crossed by the departing soul on its way to the land of the departed. Evidently the extension of the original thought to cover its seeming opposite has a basis in the nature of things. Its most elaborate presentment is in the ancient myths of the nether regions and of the seven streams that watered them—from Styx that with nine-fold weary wanderings bounded Tartarus, to where

> "Far off from these, a slow and silent stream,
> Letho the river of oblivion runs."

Nor has Christianity disdained to adapt the idea.

158

Rivers and Death

Bunyan, for example, brings his two pilgrims within sight of the heavenly City. " Now I saw further that between them and the gate was a river ; but there was no bridge, and the river was very deep. At the sight therefore of this river, the pilgrims were much stunned ; but the men that went with them said, you must go through or you cannot come at the gate."

What suggestive power has the river to induce this more sombre train of reflection ? Surely that embodied in the old proverb—Follow the river and you will come to the sea. Clough, in his little poem, " The Stream of Life," concludes with a note of sadness, almost of despair :

> " O end to which all currents tend,
>   Inevitable sea,
> To which we flow, what do we know,
>   What shall we guess of thee ?
>
> A roar we hear upon thy shore,
>   As we our course fulfil ;
> Scarce we divine a sun will shine
>   And be above us still."

The rushing rapid and the plunging waterfall have an influence all their own in rousing intuitions of more than human life and power. The dazzling and dashing rainbows of spray appeal to the sense of sight—the internal rhythmic sound from the lighter tones which are flung around like notes from a Ström Karl's magic harp, or the alluring song of a Lorelei, to the thunder of a Niagara, nature's diapason sounding the lowest note that

159

mortal ears can catch, appeal to the sense of hearing—and underlying all is a vague sense of irresistible power. How touching, how profoundly true, the story in " Eckehard " of the little lad and his sister who wandered off until they came to the Rheinfal. There, gazing at the full sweep of that magnificent fall the little fellow throws into the swirling emerald of the waters at his feet a golden goblet, as an offering to the God whom he felt to be so near. Unconsciously he was a natural mystic. Movement, sound, and colour combined to produce in him, what it should produce in all, a sense of immanent Reality, self-moving, self-sustained. And yet even a waterfall may suggest far other thoughts—a downward course from the freshness of the uplands of youth to the broadening stream of manhood declining towards old age and the final plunge. The fall itself would thus convey vague feelings of loss of power and vigour—a loss that gathers speed as it approaches the end. So in Campbell's well-known " River of Life " :

> " When joys have lost their bloom and breath
>   And life itself is vapid,
> Why, as we reach the Falls of Death,
>   Feel we its course more rapid ? "

If so sad a train of reflections can be stimulated by the rapids and the falls of rivers, how much more so by their ending in the ocean ! Old age and death can hardly fail to assert themselves in

Rivers and Death

the minds of those who sail down some noble
river and meditate :

> " As the banks fade dimmer away,
> As the stars come out, and the night wind
>   Brings up the stream
> Murmurs and scents of the infinite sea."

Granting that the river's merging in the sea
suggests the close of life as we know it here, must
we also grant that the natural-mystic must give
way to a partial, if not an absolute, tendency to
pessimism ? That a natural-mystic should be a
pessimist would seem to be an anomaly. For he
holds that he can hold living communion with
the Real ; and such communion would carry with
it, surely, a strong hope, if not a conviction, that
change in material form cannot affect the inner
being, call it the spiritual essence, of which that
form is a particular manifestation. Deny that
nature has a soul and optimism becomes a ghastly
mockery. Believe that nature and man are linked
together as kindred forms of spiritual existence,
and then, though there will not indeed be formal
proof of immortality, there will be intuitive trust
in the future. What the implications of such a
trust may be is for the various philosophies and
theologies to determine ; but taken at its lowest
value, it would secure a man from pessimism.

In the light of these general observations, let
us consider the particular case now presented.
The river is merged in the sea—it is absorbed—its
existence as a river is terminated. But the " sub-

M   161

Nature Mysticism

stance " of its being remains ; diffused in a vaster whole, but not lost. What is this vaster whole? If we regard it as an Absolute, there may perchance be ground for pessimism. If, with certain scientists, we stop short at the conservation of energy, there is nothing ahead but a blank. But if we hold to the conservation of values, as at least a parallel to this conservation of energy, we are impelled to hold also to the conservation of all that is ultimate in individualities. For values imply modes of being which can allow of the experience of values as such. And the Nature-Mystic's direct communion with his environment is seen to be one mode by which the individual centre of life learns to live increasingly in the life of the Whole—the total Reality. There is, then, no absorption where values are conserved, but an ever richer content of experience, an ever deepening insight into its significance, and an ever keener enjoyment of the material it affords.

As a specific case of an optimistic creed based on an intuition of the essential kinship of all things, it is profitable to study the poetry of a Sufi mystic of the thirteenth century. How delicate the thought enshrined in the following lines :

" When man passed from the plant to the animal state,
He had no remembrance of his state as a plant,
Except the inclination he felt for the world of plants,
Especially at the time of spring and sweet flowers."

What is this but an anticipation of Wordsworth's " Daffodils," or even of his " Ode on Immortality " ?

Rivers and Death

The concepts and phraseology of the transmigration theory are merely temporary forms in which a deep thought clothes itself : at any rate, they are not necessary adjuncts of the thought ; nor do they preclude sympathy with the following condensed statement of this same mystic's world-philosophy :

" I died from the mineral and became a plant ;
I died from the plant and reappeared as an animal ;
I died from the animal and became a man.
Wherefore then should I fear ? When did I grow less by
    dying ?
Next time I shall die from the man
That I may grow the wings of angels.
From the angel, too, I must advance.
All things shall perish save His face."

With an insight like unto this, a mystic need not fear because the river flows into the sea ! In spite of appearances, the idea of life can still reign supreme. The river of death embodies a true insight—but of a transition only, not of an abiding state. We die to live more fully.

This sense of continuity in the flow of the stream of life, and of the abidingness of its existence through all vicissitudes has been strikingly expressed by Jefferies. He is sitting on the grass-grown tumulus where some old warrior was buried two thousand years ago, and his thought slips back over the interval. " Two thousand years being a second to the soul could not cause its extinction. . . . Resting by the tumulus, the spirit of the man who had been interred there was

163

Nature Mysticism

to me really alive, and very close. This was quite natural and simple as the grass waving in the wind, the bees humming, and the lark's songs. Only by the strongest effort of the mind could I understand the idea of extinction; that was supernatural, requiring a miracle; the immortality of the soul natural, like the earth. Listening to the sighing of the grass I felt immortality as I felt the beauty of the summer morning, and I thought beyond immortality, of other conditions, more beautiful than existence, higher than immortality."

Let Morris sum up the thoughts and emotions aroused by the mystical influences of water flowing onward to join the ocean.

" Flow on, O mystical river, flow on through desert and
        city ;
Broken or smooth flow onward into the Infinite sea.
Who knows what urges thee on ?

    .   .   .   .   .   .

Surely we know not at all, but the cycle of Being is
        eternal,
Life is eternal as death, tears are eternal as joy.
As the stream flowed it will flow ; though 'tis sweet,
        yet the sea will be bitter ;
Foul it with filth, yet the Deltas grow green and the ocean
        is clear.
Always the sun and the winds will strike its broad
        surface and gather
Some purer drops from its depths to float in the clouds
        of the sky ;—
Soon these shall fall once again, and replenish the full-
        flowing river.
Roll round then, O mystical circle ! flow onward, ineffable
        stream ! "

CHAPTER XXII

THE OCEAN

THE Ocean ! What is its mystic significance ? A question as fraught with living issues as its physical object is spacious and profound. Infinitely varied and yet unchanging; gentle and yet terrible; radiant and yet awful;

> "Calm or convulsed, in breeze, or gale, or storm,
> Icing the pole, or in the torrid clime
> Dark heaving "—

there is not a mood with which the ocean cannot link itself, nor a problem to which it cannot hint, albeit darkly, a solution. To attempt a description of its external phenomena were a hardy task— much more to grapple with its protean influences on the souls of men.

Let the approach be by way of mythology. It was shown how that Thales was partly guided to his choice of Water as the *Welt-stoff* by its place and function in the ancient cosmologies. Numerous and widely diffused were the myths of a primeval ocean out of which the structured universe arose. The Babylonian tablet tells of the time before the times " when above were not raised the heavens, and below on the earth a plant had not grown up ;

165

Nature Mysticism

the abyss also had not broken up its boundary. The chaos, the sea, was the producing mother of them all." A passage from the Rig Veda speaks likewise of the time, or rather the no-time, which preceded all things. "Death was not then, nor immortality; there was no distinction of day or night. Only *Something* breathed without breath, inwardly turned towards itself. Other than it there was nothing." And how did these ancient mystics best picture to themselves the primeval, or timeless, *Something?*—"What was the veiling cover of everything?"—they themselves ask. And they answer with another question—"Was it the water's deep abyss?" They think of it as "an ocean without light." "Then (say they) from the nothingness enveloped in empty gloom, Desire (Love) arose, which was the first germ of mind. This loving impulse the Sages, seeking in their heart, recognised as the bond between Being and Non-Being." How deep the plunge here into the sphere of abstract thought! Yet so subtle and forceful had been the mystic influence of the ocean on the primitive mind that it declares itself as a working element in their abstrusest speculations.

Nor has this mystic influence as suggesting the mysteries of origin ceased to be operative. Here is Tennyson, addressing his new-born son :

"Out of the deep, my child, out of the deep."

And again, when nearing the end of his own life, he strikes the same old mystic chord :

The Ocean

" When that which drew from out tho boundless deep
      Turns again home."

Wordsworth, of course, felt the power of this ocean
born intuition, and assures us that here and now :

" Tho' inland far wo bo,
   Our souls have sight of that immortal sea
   Which brought us hither."

And of intense interest as modernising the ancient
concept of " *Something* which breathed without
breath," is his appeal :

" Liston, tho mighty Being is awake,
   And doth with his eternal motion mako
   A sound like thunder—everlastingly."

It will not be possible to do more than draw
attention to those chief characteristics of the ocean
which have given it so large a place in the minds of
men. And first would come the vastness of the
sea, which prompts vague intuitions of mystery
and infinity. The sight of its limitless expanse still
has this power. " The sea (says Holmes) belongs
to eternity, and not to time, and of that it sings for
ever and ever." How natural, then, the trend of
the mythology just mentioned, and the belief in
a primeval ocean—a formless abyss—Tiâmat—
which, as Milton puts it in a splendid line, is :

"The womb of nature and perhaps her grave."

But added to the mystic influence of sheer limit-
lessness are the manifestations of power and
majesty, which compel the awe and wonder of those

Nature Mysticism

who " go down to the sea in ships and do their
business in great waters." In the minds of early
navigators, the experience of the terrors of the
sea begot a sense of relationship to hostile powers.
One of the oldest Aryan words for sea, the German
Meer, Old English *Mere*, means death or destruction; and the destructive action of the ocean's
untutored elementary force found personifications
in the Teutonic Oegir (Terror), with his dreaded
daughter, and the sea-goddess, Ran, his wife, who
raged in storms and overwhelmed the ships. The
eastern peoples, including the Hebrews, regarded
the sea as the abode of evil powers, as certain of
the visions in the Book of Daniel strikingly testify.
Nor is this feeling of the action of hostile powers
yet extinct. Victor Hugo makes fine use of it in
his description of the storm in " The Toilers of the
Sea."

Jefferies was always deeply affected by the vastness and strength of the sea.. " Let me launch
forth " (he writes) " and sail over the rim of the sea
yonder, and when another rim rises over that, and
again onwards into an ever-widening ocean of
idea and life. For with all the strength of the
wave, and its succeeding wave, the depth and race
of the tide, the clear definition of the sky; with
all the subtle power of the great sea, there rises the
equal desire. Give me life strong and full as the
brimming ocean; give me thoughts wide as its
plain. . . . My soul rising to the immensity utters
its desire-prayer with all the strength of the sea."

The Ocean

In many of its aspects, the ocean can stimulate and soften moods of sadness. The peculiar potency of the play of the waves is reserved for the next chapter. But the more general influences of this character are many and of undoubted significance. The vast loneliness of its watery, restless plains ; its unchangeableness ; its seeming disregard for human destinies ; the secrets buried under its heaving waters—these and a multitude of like phenomena link themselves on to man's sadder reveries. Morris asks :

> " Peace, moaning sea ; what tale have you to tell,
> What mystic tidings, all unknown before ? "

His answer is in terms of longing for the unrealised :

> " The voice of yearning, deep but scarce expressed,
>   For something which is not, but may be yet ;
>   Too full of sad continuance to forget,
> Too troubled with desires to be at rest,
> Too self-conflicting ever to be blest."

In strong contrast with this is the exhilarating, tonic power of the sea. Coleridge, revisiting the seashore, cries :

> " God be with thee, gladsome Ocean !
>   How gladly greet I thee once more."

Myers emphasises the fact that Swinburne, in his principal autobiographical poem, "Thalassius, or Child of the Sea," reveals a nature for which the elemental play of the ocean is the intensest stimulus. The author of that poem tells how once he

169

wandered off into indulgence of personal feelings, and how his mother, the sea, recalled him from such wanderings to

> "charm him from his own soul's separate sense
> With infinite and invasive influence,
> That made strength sweet in him and sweetness strong,
> Being now no more a singer, but a song."

And akin to this exhilarating effect on a poet's sensibility is that which it has exercised on the large scale in moulding the characters and fortunes of seafaring nations.   Longfellow had a firm grip of this historical fact :

> "Wouldst thou (so the helmsman answered)
> Learn the secret of the sea ?
> Only those who brave its dangers
> Comprehend its mystery."

Allan Cunningham's sea songs furnish the classical expression of the spirit in its modern guise as embodied in the British sailor—the defender of the isle that is "compassed by the inviolate sea" :

> "The sea ! the sea ! the open sea !
> The ever fresh, the ever free."

Byron may be criticised as too consciously "posing" in his well-known apostrophe to the ocean ; nevertheless it contains a tang of the Viking spirit :

> "And I have loved thee, Ocean ! and my joy
> Of youthful sports was on thy breast to be
> Borne like thy bubbles onward : from a boy
> I wantoned with thy breakers."

The Ocean

What is the core of this Viking buoyancy and exhilaration ? Surely a sense of freedom, inspired by a life on the ocean, and fostered by the very hardships and dangers which that life entails.

Thus cumulative is the evidence that the present, for all its materialism, inherits the essence of the ancient mysticism ; or rather, it is open to the same impulses and intuitions, however changed and changing the forms they may assume. On the one hand, the infinite complexity of man's developing soul-life ; on the other, the limitless range of the moods and aspects of the ocean : the two are spiritually linked by ultimate community of nature : deep calls to deep : the response is living and eternal.

CHAPTER XXIII

WAVES

THE most familiar appeal of the Ocean is that of the wave which speeds over its surface or breaks upon its shores. Poets have found here an inexhaustible theme. Painters have here expended their utmost skill. Whether it is the tiny ripple that dies along the curving sands, or the merry, rustling, crested surf that hurries on to wanton in the rocky pools, or the storm billow that rushes wildly against an iron-bound coast to spurt aloft its sheets of spray or to hurl its threatening mass on the trembling strand—in each and every form the wave is a moving miracle. Through every change of contour and interplay of curves, its lines are ever of inimitable grace. Its gradations of colour, its translucent opalescence framed in gleaming greens and tender greys, wreathed with the radiance of the foam, are of inimitable charm. Its gamuts of sounds, the faint lisp of the wavelet on the pebbly beach, the rhythmic rise and fall of the plashing or plunging surf, the roar and scream of the breaker, and the boom of the billow, are of inimitable range. What marvel is it that even the commonplace of the sons of men yield themselves

172

Waves

gladly to a spell they cannot analyse, content to linger, to gaze, and to ponder !

If the spell of the waves enthralls the ordinary mortal, how much more those whose æsthetic and spiritual senses are keen and disciplined ? Coleridge, while listening to the tide, with eyes closed, but with mind alert, finds his thoughts wandering back to

> " that blind bard who on the Chian strand
> By those deep sounds possessed with inward light,
> Beheld the Iliad and the Odyssee
> Rise to the swelling of the voiceful sea."

Swinburne, listening to the same music, exclaims :

> " Yea, surely the sea like a harper
> Laid his hand on the shore like a lyre."

Sometimes the emphasis is on the sympathy with the striving forces manifested in the ceaseless activity of the ocean as it

> " beats against the stern dumb shore
> The stormy passion of its mighty heart."

Sometimes the emphasis is on the subjective mood which that activity arouses :

> " Break, break, break,
> On thy cold gray stones, O sea.
> And I would that my tongue could utter
> The thoughts that arise in me."

Sometimes the two are indissolubly blended as in the song, " Am Meer," so exquisitely set to music by Schubert—where the rhythmic echoes of the

heaving tide accompany the surging emotions of a
troubled heart.

The direct impression made by the objective
phenomena of the play of waves finds abundant
expression in the whole range of literature—not
the least forcefully in Tennyson. How fine his
painting of the wave on the open sea.

" As a wild wave in the wide North-Sea
　Green glimmering towards the summit, bears, with all
　Its stormy crests that smoke against the skies,
　Down on a bark, and overbears the bark,
　And him that helms it."

How perfect also the description of a wave breaking
on a level, sandy beach :

" The crest of some slow-arching wave,
Heard in dead night along that table-shore,
Drops flat, and after the great waters break
Whitening for half a league, and thin themselves,
Far over sands marbled with moon and cloud,
From less and less to nothing."

As to the moods thus stimulated, the one most
frequently provoked would seem to be that of
sadness. Or would it be truer to say that those
whose thoughts are tinged with melancholy, or
weighted with sorrow, find in the restless, endless
tossing and breaking of the waves their fittest
companions ?

How sad this passage from the French poet-
philosopher, Guyot. " I remember that once,
sitting on the beach, I watched the serried waves

Waves

rolling towards me. They came without interruption from the expanse of the sea, roaring and white. Beyond the one dying at my feet I noticed another; and farther behind that one, another; and farther still another and another—a multitude. At last, as far as I could see, the whole horizon seemed to rise and roll on towards me. There was a reservoir of infinite, inexhaustible forces there. How deeply I felt the impotency of man to arrest the effort of that whole ocean in movement! A dike might break one of the waves; it could break hundreds and thousands of them; but would not the immense and indefatigable ocean gain the victory? And this rising tide seemed to me the image of the whole of nature assailing humanity, which vainly wishes to direct its course, to dam it in, to master it. Man struggles bravely; he multiplies his efforts. Sometimes he believes himself to be the conqueror. That is because he does not look far enough ahead, and because he does not notice far out on the horizon the great waves which, sooner or later, must destroy his work and carry himself away."

Similar is the train of thought which finds poetical expression in Matthew Arnold's "Dover Beach."

> "Come to the window, sweet is the night-air!
> Only, from the long line of spray
> Where the sea meets the moon-blanched land
> Listen! you hear the grating roar
> Of pebbles which the waves draw back and fling,
> At their return, up the high strand,

175

Nature Mysticism

Begin, and cease, and then again begin,
With tremulous cadence slow, and bring
The eternal note of sadness in.

. . . .

Sophocles heard it long ago,
Heard it on the Ægœan, and it brought
Into his mind the turbid ebb and flow
Of human misery ; we
Find also in the sound a thought ;
Hearing it by this distant northern sea."

And the thought ! " The melancholy, long, with-
drawing roar " of the Sea of Faith, retreating down
the " naked shingles of the world ! "

But if the pessimistic mood may thus find support in watching the waves of the sea, so no less
surely can the hopeful and joyous mood be evolved
and stimulated by the same influence. Before
Sophocles came Æschylus. The greatest hero of
this earlier poet was Prometheus, the friend of
man, who, tortured but unshaken, looked out from
his Caucasian rock on the presentments of primeval
nature. How sublime his appeal !

" Ether of heaven, and Winds untired of wing,
Rivers whose fountains fail not, and thou Sea
Laughing in waves innumerable ! "

To him the winds and waves brought a message
of untiring, indomitable energy—the movement,
the gleam, inspired fresh life and hope. The ideas
immanent in the ocean wave are as varied as the
human experiences to which they are akin.

Or take another group of these ideas immanent

176

Waves

in the phenomena of the wave—the group which rouse and nurture the æsthetic side of man's nature. Very significant in this regard is the fact that not for the Greeks alone, but also for the Hindus and the Teutons, the goddesses of beauty were wave-born. When Aphrodite walked the earth, flowers sprang up beneath her feet; but her birthplace was the crest of a laughing wave. So Kama, the Hindu Cupid, and the Apsaras, lovely nymphs, rose from the wind-stirred surface of the sea, drawn upward in streaming mists by the ardent sun. So, too, the Teutonic Freyja took shape in the sea-born cloudlets of the upper air.

The loveliness of the wave, dancing, tossing, or breaking must have entered, from earliest days, deeply into the heart and imagination of man, and have profoundly influenced his mythology, his art, and his poetry. We trace this influence in olden days by the myths of Poseidon with his sea-horses and the bands of Tritons, Nereids, and Oceanides—each and all giving substance to vague intuitions and subconscious perceptions of the physical beauty of the ocean.

And as for our own more immediate forefathers, the mystic spell of the ocean wave sank deep into their rugged souls. " When you so dance " (says Shakespeare to a maiden) " I wish you a wave o' the sea, that you might ever do nothing but that." The experiences of countless watchers of the wave went to the framing of that wish !

And, as has been richly proved by quotations

Nature Mysticism

from our modern poets, the mystic spell gains in potency as man's æsthetic powers are keener and more disciplined. The present-day nature-mystic needs no imaginary personifications to bring him into communion with the beauty, the mystery, of the ocean wave. He conceives of it as a manifestation of certain modes of being which are akin to himself and which speak to him in language too plain to be ignored or misinterpreted. Human knowledge has not yet advanced far enough to define more closely such modes of experience ; but the fact of the experience remains.

CHAPTER XXIV

STILL WATERS

Tiefer Stille herrscht im Wasser,
Ohne Regung ruht das Meer,
Und bekümmert sieht der Schiffer
Glatte Fläche rings umher.

Keine Luft von keiner Seite !
Todesstille fürchterlich !
In der ungeheuern Weite
Reget keine Welle sich.

Thus does Goethe, in this little poem of two verses, with a masterly ease that carries conviction, suggest to us the subtle power of a calm at sea. The mountain tarn, alone with the sky, has a charm that is all its own. The shining levels of the lake, in the lower hollows of the hills ; the quiet reaches of a river where the stream seems to pause and gather strength for its onward course ; even the still pool that hides in the meadows among the alders and willows : each of these has its own peculiar charm—a charm which is hard to analyse but almost universal in its range of appeal. But potent above them all is this Meeresstille, this

179

Nature Mysticism

calm at sea—when, as Bowring finely translates Goethe's second verse:

"Not a zephyr is in motion!
Silence fearful as the grave!
In the mighty waste of ocean
Sunk to rest is every wave."

Turner, in his "Liber Studiorum," attempted to depict a calm at sea. The picture is not one of his most successful efforts: but so great an artist could not fail to seize on the essential features of his subject. The sun is heralding his advent by flinging upward athwart the mists and cloudlets a stream of diffused light which fills the scene with a soft pervading glow. The surface of the water is glassy, not much more substantial than the haze which floats above it. But deep as is the calm, old ocean cannot quite forget his innate restlessness; he gently urges onward a succession of slow risings and fallings, with broad ripples to mark their boundaries, and to tell of spent billows and far-heaving tides. The movement of the waters is, as it were, subconsciously felt rather than perceived; or, if perceived, it is lost in the pervading sense of placid spaciousness. The boats and their occupants, so far from disturbing the sense of calm, are made to enhance it. And the unruffled surface of the water is rendered palpably impalpable by the magic of reflections.

180

Still Waters

Morris has given us a word-picture of similar import.

" Oh, look ! the sea is fallen asleep,
    The sail hangs idle evermore ;
Yet refluent from the outer deep
    The low wave sobs upon the shore.
Silent the dark cave ebbs and fills
    Silent the broad woods wave and sway ;
    Yet yonder fairy fringe of spray
Is born of surges vast as hills."

Jefferies gives us a companion picture of a calm sea in full sunshine. " Immediately in front dropped the deep descent of the bowl-like hollow which received and brought up to me the faint sound of the summer waves. Yonder lay the immense plain of the sea, the palest green under the continued sunshine, as though the heat had evaporated the colour from it ; there was no distinct horizon, a heat-mist inclosed it, and looked farther away than the horizon would have done."

In each of these seascapes, the same essential features find a place—the calm expanse without any defined boundary—the silence—the play of delicate colour—the suggestions of rest after toil, of peace after storm—and chiefest of all, the strangely moving contrast of power and gentleness, the suggestion of hidden strength. Doubtless we have in these the secret of much of the mystic influence of the mighty ocean in its serenest moods ;

Nature Mysticism

doubtless we have in these the manifestations of immanent ideas which have subtle power to subdue the human soul to pensive thought and unwonted restfulness.

Not unlike them in general character and function, save for the element of vastness, are the influences immanent in the calm of evening or night landscapes. Goethe has an exquisite fragment which is a fitting pendent to his Meeres-stille :

> Ueber allen Gipfeln
> Ist Ruh,
> In allen Wipfeln
> Spürest du
> Kaum einen Hauch ;
> Die Vögelein schweigen im Walde.
> Warte nur, balde
> Ruhest du auch.

Thus translated by Bowring :

> " Hush'd on the hill
>   Is the breeze ;
> Scarce by the zephyr
>   The trees
> Softly are pressed ;
> The woodbird's asleep on the bough.
> Wait, then, and thou
> Soon wilt find rest."

Who does not sympathise, in the measure possible to him, with Wordsworth's interpretations and premonitions ?

Still Waters

> " It is a beauteous Evening, calm and free,
> The holy time is quiet as a Nun
> Breathless with adoration ; the broad sun
> Is sinking down in its tranquillity ;
> The gentleness of heaven is on the sea."

And a less well-known passage :

> " Thine is the tranquil hour, purpureal eve,
> But long as godlike wish, or hope divine,
> Informs my spirit, ne'er can I believe
> That this magnificence is wholly thine !
> —From worlds not quickened by the sun
> A portion of the gift is won."

Yes, the nature-mystic might well be content to rest his case on the influences of a calm at sea or a peaceful sunset. These will maintain their power as long as there are human eyes to see and human emotions to be stirred.

Not the least of the charms of still water is one which was mentioned in the description of Turner's picture—the charm of reflections. And here we discover a fresh vein of Nature Mysticism. As Hawthorne says, there is " no fountain so small but that heaven may be reflected in its bosom." Nay, as painters well know, the very puddles in a country lane, or in a London street, may be transfigured by thus reflecting lights and colours, and become indispensable factors in a composition.

The phenomena of perfect reflection are often of exceptional beauty. How perfect the effect of Wordsworth's lines :

> " The swan on sweet St. Mary's Lake
> Floats double, swan and shadow."

183

Nature Mysticism

And, more generally, of another lake :

> " The mere
> Seems firm as solid crystal, breathless, clear,
> And motionless ; and, to the gazer's eye,
> Deeper than ocean, in the immensity
> Of its vague mountains and unreal sky."

So on the broad, slowly moving waters of peaty
rivers, the reflections of sky and landscape seem
almost to exceed the originals in lustre and delicate
detail. Some of the Tasmanian rivers possess this
reflecting quality in an exceptional degree.

Nor are the phenomena of broken reflections
inferior in beauty and suggestion. Instead of
motionless repetition of given detail, there are
flickering, sinuous, mazy windings and twistings
of colour, light, and shadow—a capricious hurrying
from surface to surface. Knowledge of optics
cannot rob them of their marvel and their glamour.
And if such be their effect on the modern mind,
what must it have been on that of primitive man !
No laws of reflection came within his ken. He
looked down on the still surface of tarn, or pool,
or fountain, and saw, sinking downwards, another
world, another sky, losing themselves in mystery.
Mere wonder would yield place to meditation.
Ah ! what secrets must lurk in those crystal
depths, if only one could surprise them—wrest
them from the beings who inhabit that nether
realm ! Possibly even the world-riddle might so
be solved ! And thus it came to pass that most

184

Still Waters

water spirits were deemed to be dowered with prophetic gifts.

The Teutonic water-gods were " wise "—they could foretell the future. In classical mythology, Proteus, the old man of the sea, presents himself as a well-developed embodiment of this belief. Old Homer knew how to use the material thus provided, and Virgil, in his choicest manner, follows the lead so given. In the fourth book of the Georgics, Aristæus, who had lost his bees, in despair appealed to his mother, the river-nymph, Cyrene. She bids him consult Proteus, the old prophet of the sea. He follows her counsel, captures Proteus, and compels him to tell the cause of his trouble. " The seer at last constrained by force, rolled on him eyes fierce-sparkling with grey light, and gnashing his teeth in wrath, opened his lips to speak the oracles of fate."

Once more the transient must be allowed to fall away, and the central intuition be recognised and grasped. The sense of a secret to be gained, of a mystery to be revealed—of a broken reflection of some fuller world—has been nurtured by the reflections of form and light and colour in nature's mirror. The older, simpler impressions made by such phenomena persist with deeper meanings. The " natural " emotion they stimulate affords the kind of sustenance on which Nature Mysticism can thrive. Longfellow, in his poem, " The Bridge," strikes the deeper note. The rushing water draws the poet's reflections away from

185

Nature Mysticism

a world of imperfection to the sphere of the ideal.

> " And for ever and for ever,
>   As long as the river flows,
>   As long as the heart has passions,
>   As long as life has woes ;
>
> The moon and its broken reflection
>   And its shadows shall appear,
> As the symbol of love in heaven
>   And its wavering image here."

And thus the mountain tarn, the placid lake, the quiet river reaches, the hidden pool, and the ocean at rest, have each and all their soul language, and can speak to man as a sharer of soul-nature. Well might the Hebrew psalmist give us one of the marks of the Divine Shepherd—"He leadeth me beside the still waters."

CHAPTER XXV

ANAXIMENES AND THE AIR

HITHERTO our attention has been almost exclusively fixed upon the mystical influences of water in motion or at rest. And even though we went no farther afield, a fair presentment has been gained of what a modern nature-mystic might advance in explanation and defence of his characteristic views and modes of experience. We now turn to consider other ranges of physical phenomena, which, though of equal dignity and significance, will not meet with equal fullness of treatment—otherwise the limits proposed for this study would be seriously exceeded.

We have seen how and why Thales deemed water to be the *Welt-stoff*. His immediate successors, while adhering to his principles and aims, were not content with his choice. They successively sought for something less material. One of them, Anaximenes, was attracted by the qualities and functions of the atmosphere, and his speculations will serve as an introduction to the mysticism of winds and storms and clouds. Only a single statement of his is preserved in its original form ; but fortunately it is full of signifi-

187

Nature Mysticism

cance. "As our soul" (said the sage), "which is air, holds us together, so wind and air encompass the whole world." This, interpreted in the light of ancient comments, shows that Anaximenes compared the breath of life to the air, and regarded the two as essentially related—indeed as identical. For the breath, he thought, holds together both animal and human life; and so the air holds together the whole world in a complex unity. He reached the wider doctrine by observing that the air is, to all appearance, infinitely extended, and that earth, water, and fire seem to be but islands in an ocean which spreads around them on all sides, penetrating their inmost pores, and bathing their smallest atoms. It was on such facts and appearances that he based his main doctrine. If we think of the modern theory of the luminiferous ether, we shall not be far from his view-point. But the simpler and more obvious qualities of the air would of course not be without their influence —its mobility and incessant motion; its immateriality; its inexhaustibility; its seeming eternity. It is, therefore, not astonishing that with his attention thus focussed on a group of truly wonderful phenomena, the old nature-philosopher should have selected air as his primary substance— as the universal vehicle of vital and psychic force.

It is of especial interest to the nature-mystic to find that Anaximenes was faithful to the doctrine that the primary substance must contain in itself the cause of its own motion. And the interest is in-

Anaximenes and the Air

tensified in view of the fact that his insistence on the life-giving properties of air rests on a widely spread group of animistic notions which have exercised an extraordinary influence on the world at large. Let Tylor furnish a summary. "Hebrew shows *nephesh*, 'breath,' passing into all the meanings of life, soul, mind, animal, while *ruach* and *neshamah* make the like transition from 'breath' to 'spirit'; and to these the Arabic *nefs* and *ruh* correspond. The same is the history of the Sanskrit âtman and prâna, of Greek *psyche* and *pneuma*, of Latin *anima, animus, spiritus*. So Slavonic *duch* has developed the meaning of 'breath' into that of 'soul' or 'spirit'; and the dialects of the gypsies have this word *duk* with the meanings of 'breath, spirit, ghost,' whether these pariahs brought the word from India as part of their inheritance of Aryan speech, or whether they adopted it in their migration across Slavonic lands. German *geist* and English *ghost*, too, may possibly have the same original sense of breath." How marvellously significant this ascent from the perceptions of wind and breath to what we now understand by soul and spirit! The most attenuated concepts have their basis in the physical world. Even to this present day, as Max Müller remarks, "the soul or the spirit remains a breath, an airy breath, for this is the least material image of the soul which they can conceive."

Another doctrine of Anaximenes is most worthy of note by nature mystics, as well as by scientists.

Nature Mysticism

It is well stated by Theophrastus. " The air differs in rarity and in density as the nature of things is different ; when very attenuated it becomes fire, when more condensed, wind, and then cloud ; and when still more condensed, water and earth and stone ; and all other things are composed of these ; and he regards motion as eternal, and by this changes are produced." We have here a distinct adumbration of the atomic theory in its most defensible form—that is to say, a conception which makes the differences in various substances consist in differences in condensation or rarefaction of the particles of the primary substance. The simple normal condition of this substance he deemed to be air. In its rarefied condition, it becomes fire, and in its condensed condition it progresses by stages from liquid to solid. And just as the modern chemist is beginning to have good ground for believing that all substances, or so-called elements, may be the result of a series of differentiations and compositions of an originally homogeneous substance, in spite of the fact that he is not yet able to effect the transformations in his laboratory, so, all those centuries ago, the Milesian sage seized on the same root idea and made it the basis of a world philosophy. It is a long cry from the old idea, familiar to Homer, that mist or vapour is condensed air to the cosmology of a Herbert Spencer, and yet nature is so rich in material for prompting intuitions of her deepest truths that one ultimate cause of material evolu-

Anaximenes and the Air

tion was revealed in days when science was hardly brought to the birth.

An examination, albeit cursory and partial, of this ancient speculation, has thus revealed at any rate two results of prime importance in the study of Nature Mysticism. The one is that the air has furnished the primary type of the soul as the principle of life—man's fleeting breath has suggested and fostered the idea of immortality; the wind that bloweth where it listeth, the idea of a realm of changeless spirit! The other result is that certain of nature's most obvious phenomena, when seized by intuition, can supply a key to some of her profoundest secrets. Shall not these results be as true for the world of to-day as for the flourishing times of old-world Miletus?

CHAPTER XXVI

WINDS AND CLOUDS

THE recognition of the mystic element in external
nature has had its fluctuations in most ages and
climes, and not least so in England. Marvel, in
his day, felt the numbness creeping on that comes
of divorce from nature, and uttered his plaint of
" The Mower against Gardens."

> " 'Tis all enforced, the fountain and the grot,
> While the sweet fields do lie forgot,
> Where willing nature does to all dispense
> A wild and fragrant innocence."

And declared of the polished statues made to adorn
the gardens, that

> " howsoe'er the figures do excel,
> The gods themselves with us do dwell."

His protests, however, did not avail to ward off
the artificiality of the reign of Pope. Here are
two lines from the " Essay on Man."

> " Lo, the poor Indian ! whose untutored mind
> Sees God in clouds, or hears Him in the wind."

" Untutored ! " The poor Indian could have
taught Pope many things, and perhaps made a
nobler man of him ! For the poetry and mystic

192

Winds and Clouds

influence of the winds were experienced and expressed with a fullness of experience and feeling to which the town-bred poet was all too great a stranger. The range, the beauty and vigour of the myth of the four winds as developed among the native races of America (says Tylor) had scarcely a rival elsewhere in the mythology of the world. They evolved " the mystic quaternion "— the wild and cruel North Wind—the lazy South, the lover—the East Wind, the morning bringer— and the West, Mudjekeewis, the father of them all. Outside the quaternion were the dancing Pauppukkeewis, the Whirlwind, and the fierce and shifty hero, Monobozho, the North-West Wind. The spirit of these legends, if not their accurate detail, can be appreciated in Longfellow's " Hiawatha."

The magnificent imagery of the Hebrew psalmists should have given to Pope at least a touch of sympathy with " the untutored mind " ; for they love to represent God making " the winds His messengers," or as Himself " flying on the wings of the wind." Or the prophet Ezekiel could have brought home to him some of the deeper thoughts that the winds have stirred in the soul of man. " Then said he unto me, Prophesy unto the wind, prophesy, son of man, and say to the wind: . . . Come from the four winds, O breath, and breathe upon these slain, that they may live." The Indian undoubtedly lacked tuition, but not exactly of the kind his would-be tutor could bestow.

Nature Mysticism

Man, says Browning,

> " imprints for ever
> His presence on all lifeless things : the winds
> Are henceforth voices, wailing or a shout,
> A querulous mutter, or a quick gay laugh."

That is better. But why " lifeless " ? Why " imprints " ? Best is the Hebrew apostrophe—" come from the four winds, O breath, and breathe—that we may live. Give us of the life that is in you." And that is the mystic's prayer.

The winds of heaven were bound to make indelible impressions on the primitive mind. But few will be prepared for Max Müller's statement that the wind, next to fire, is the most important phenomenon in nature which has led to the conception of a divine being. But our surprise ceases when we realise how manifest and universal are the parts played by the wind in relation to man's weal or woe—they bring the rain, they drive the storm, they clear the air. The landsman knows much—the sailor more. Guy de Maupassant makes the sailor say, " Vous ne le (vent) connaissez point, gens de la terre ! Nous autres, nous le connaissons plus que notre père ou que notre mère, cet invisible, ce terrible, ce capricieux, ce sournois, ce féroce. Nous l'aimons et nous le redoutons, nous savons ses malices et ses colères . . . car la lutte entre nous et lui ne s'interrompt jamais."

Wind-gods and wind-myths are practically of world-wide diffusion. Those of the American Indians have already been noted. Similar, if less

194

Winds and Clouds

striking and poetical, are those which prevail among the Polynesians and Maoris. Those of the Greeks and Romans are best known, but have abundant parallels in other lands. The Mâruts of the Vedic hymns are unequivocally storm-gods, who uproot forests and shatter rocks—strikers, shouters, warriors—though able anon to take the form of new-born babes. The Babylonians had their wind-gods, good and bad, created in the lower part of the heaven, and joining at times in the fateful fight against the dragon. And our Teutonic fathers had their storm-gods who were brave warriors, Odin, or Wodin, being the chief. Grimm thus sums up Wodin's characteristics. "He is the all-pervading and formative power, who bestows shape and beauty on man and all things, from whom proceeds the gift of song, and the management of war and victory, on whom at the same time depends the fertility of the soil, nay, wishing and all the highest gifts and blessings." We have here a typical transition. The abstract conception of " the all-pervading creative and formative power is evidently later than that of the storm-god, rushing through the air in the midst of the howling tempest—later even than that of the god who quaffs the draught of inspiration and shares it with seers, bards, and faithful fallen warriors. The idea of life or soul emerges, and frees itself from its cruder elements ; the tempest god yields place to the All-Father, sitting on the throne of the world. The same evolution is seen in the case of the cloud-

195

compelling Zeus. Nay, Jehovah Himself would
seem to have been originally a god of storms,
sitting above the canopy of the aerial water-flood,
" making the clouds His chariot," and " walking
upon the wings of the wind," His voice the thunder,
His shaft the lightning. How strange and unexpected the transformations of these immanent
ideas ! Yet there is organic continuity throughout.

So large is the place filled by the phenomena of
the winds, that human imagination has not always
stopped short at their mere personification or
deification. In many American languages, we are
told, the same word is used for storm and for god ;
so, too, with certain tribes in Central Africa.
That is to say, the name for the storm-wind has
become the general name for deity !

But how about the present ? Can it be said that
in the present day, among civilised peoples, the
phenomena of the winds have any important part
to play ? An appeal to literature is decisive on the
point. No description of open-air life, or even of
life within doors where nature is not altogether shut
out, can pass over the emotional influences of the
winds. They sob, they moan, they sigh ; they rustle,
roar, or bellow ; they exhilarate or depress ; they
suggest many and varied trains of thought.

> " Blow, blow, thou winter wind,
> Thou art not so unkind
> As man's ingratitude "—

the connection here is not altogether based on
fancy—the biting winds of winter have their own

Winds and Clouds

emotional " tone " for susceptible minds, just as truly as the spanking breeze " that follows fast," or the balmy zephyr of summer, and have moulded modern thought in manifold and unsuspected modes. Shelley, who has been called the great laureate of the wind, contemplating the coming storm and the wild whirling of the autumn leaves, is profoundly moved and exclaims :

> " O wild West-Wind, thou breath of Autumn's being—
> . . . Be thou, spirit fierce,
> My spirit ! Be thou me, impetuous one,
> Drive my dead thoughts over the universe
> Like withered leaves to quicken a new birth."

Alexander Smith, with a spirit rendered buoyant by the blast, tells how

> " The Wind, that grand old harper, smote
> His thunder harp of pines."

Guy de Maupassant, in the passage already partly quoted, shows that the modern sailor can still personify. " Quel personnage, le vent, pour les marins ! On en parle comme d'un homme, d'un souverain tout puissant, tantôt terrible et tantôt bienveillant. . . . Aucun ennemi ne nous donne que lui la sensation du combat, ne nous force a tant de prévoyance, car il est le maître de la mer, celui qu'on peut éviter, utiliser ou fuir, mais qu'on ne dompte jamais." Kingsley breaks forth :

> " Welcome, wild North-Easter !
> Shame it is to see
> Odes to every zephyr ;
> Ne'er an ode to thee.

. . . . . .

197

Nature Mysticism

Come as came our fathers,
    Heralded by thee,
Conquering from the eastward,
    Lords by land and sea.

Come, and strong within us
    Stir the Viking's blood,
Bracing brain and sinew ;
    Blow, thou wind of God ! "

No, the power of vision is not dim, on man's part ; nor, on the part of the winds of heaven, is abated their natural power to rule men's moods as they rule the responsive ocean. Those whose mystic insight is undulled by the materialistic tendencies of the age can still have glimpses of

      " heaven's cherubim, hors'd
Upon the sightless couriers of the air."

The untutored mind of the Indian, says Pope, sees God not only in winds, but in clouds. Clouds are, so to speak, the creations of the air, and share its mystic fortunes. Even Keble could respond to their suggestion of life, and asks :

" The clouds that wrap the setting sun,
    Why, as we watch their floating wreath,
    Seem they the breath of life to breathe ? "

Wordsworth could not fail to have this experience :

" I wandered lonely as a cloud
    That floats on high o'er vales and hills."

These are genuine echoes of primitive feeling. Needless to elaborate the evidence of the ancient

198

Winds and Clouds

myths or of the beliefs of primitive peoples. Not that the evidence will not amply repay study, but that for the purpose of grasping general principles, that just adduced in the case of the winds has sufficiently served our turn. The following old Finnish prayer, however, is so fraught with significance that it would be unpardonable to pass it by. It is addressed to Ukko, the Heaven-god :

" Ukko, thou, O God above us,
  Thou, O Father in the heavens,
  Thou who rulest in the cloud-land,
  And the little cloud-lambs leadest,
  Send us down the rain from heaven,
  Make the drops to drop with honey,
  Let the drooping corn look upward,
  Let the grain with plenty rustle."

This beautiful little poem-prayer places us about midway in the development of the conscious expression of the mystic influences exercised by cloud-land. We see how, as with the winds, the clouds have played a severely practical rôle among the conditions which have rendered human life possible upon the globe. The original animistic conception of the clouds as themselves personal agents has yielded to that of a god who rules the clouds, though the animistic tendency still remains in the expression, " the little cloud-lambs." Now we have passed to the stage of modern animism which regards the clouds as a part of a vast system, the essential being of which must be described as con·sciousness.

Nature Mysticism

The chief of the ideas immanent in cloud scenery would seem to be the vagueness and unsubstantiality of its ever-changing pageantry, prompting dreams of glorious possibilities which our earthly environment is yet too gross to realise. At any rate, it is safe to assert that this constituted its main charm for the passionately visionary soul of Shelley. Study this description of a cloud-scape—one among a host which could be gathered from his poems :

> " The charm in which the sun has sunk, is shut
>   By darkest barriers of enormous cloud,
> Like mountain over mountain huddled—but
>   Growing and moving upwards in a crowd,
> And over it a space of watery blue,
> Which the keen evening star is shining through."

Or study that poem, unsurpassable of its kind, devoted wholly to this theme—especially the stanza which closes it :

> " I am the daughter of earth and water,
>   And the nursling of the sky ;
> I pass through the pores of the ocean and shores ;
>   I change, but I cannot die.
> For after the rain, when with never a stain
>   The pavilion of heaven is bare,
> And the winds and sunbeams with their convex gleams,
>   Build up the blue dome of air,
> I silently laugh at my own cenotaph,
>   And out of the caverns of rain,
> Like a child from the womb, like a ghost from the tomb
>   I arise and unbuild it again."

How crammed are these lines with the purest

200

Winds and Clouds

Nature Mysticism as moderns understand it! The sense of living process reigns supreme. They are the offspring, not of fancy, nor even of imagination as ordinarily conceived—but of insight, of vision, of living communion with a living world.

It is tempting, while dealing with the airy realms of cloud-land, to dwell at length on the mystic influence of the queen of aerial phenomena—the rainbow. That influence in the past has been immense; it still is, and ever will be, a power to be reckoned with. Science cannot rob it of its glories. The gold-winged Iris of Homer, swifter-footed than the wind, has passed. The Genesis story of " the bow in the cloud " may dissolve in the alembic of criticism—but the rainbow itself remains, still a sevenfold bridge of souls from this solid-seeming earth to a rarer land beyond. Who is there who cannot sympathise with Wordsworth?

> " My heart leaps up when I behold
>   A rainbow in the sky.
> So was it when I was a child ;
>   So it is now I am a man ;
> So let it be when I am old—
>   Or let me die."

Tempting is it also to treat of the birds—the denizens of the air—to comment on the exquisite trio of bird-poems, Wordsworth's " Cuckoo," Shelley's " Ode to a Skylark," and Keats' " Ode to a Nightingale." For assuredly it is the medium in which these delicate creatures pass their lives that gives them the chiefest share of their magic

201

and their mystery. But this gem from Victor Hugo must suffice for all the tuneful choir :

" Like a songbird be thou on life's bough,
　Lifting thy lay of love.
So sing to its shaking,
So spring at its breaking,
　Into the heaven above."

The dome of air thus expands into the dome of heaven with its eternal fires, and bids us turn to the third of the ancient sages whose speculations are aiding our steps in this tentative study.

CHAPTER XXVII

HERACLEITUS AND THE COSMIC FIRE

HERACLEITUS is a philosopher whose speculations are of surpassing interest for the student of Nature Mysticism. He was born about 540 B.C., at Ephesus, and lived some sixty years. He was one of the most remarkable thinkers of antiquity, and the main substance of his teaching remains as a living and stimulating element in the most advanced scientific and metaphysical doctrines of the present day. But taking the point of view of the nature-mystic, he derives his special significance from the manner of his early training, and from the source of his early inspirations.

While still a youth, he forsook the bustle of the city for the solitude and charm of the lovely country which surrounded his home, and he definitely set himself to feed his imagination on the concrete and sensuous imagery of the poets. He laid himself open to the impressions and intuitions which such an environment so richly provided, and thus laid the foundation for those speculations on the nature of the universe and of life which have rendered his influence so lasting and his fame so great.

He is undoubtedly difficult to understand, and

his cryptic utterances earned for him the doubtful title of the Dark. But his champions have pointed out that his obscurity of diction was not the outcome of pride or intentional assumption of mystery, but of the genuine difficulty he found in giving expression to his novel thoughts. He waxes vehement in his struggles to subdue his language to his purposes, his vague intuitions, his movements in worlds not fully realised; and in this regard he can at any rate claim the sympathy of mystics of every school.

Such was the man and such his training. What was his central, dominating thought? What was his conception of the universal Ground of existence? It was this—Pure Fire—motion is the secret of the eternal change which characterises all known phenomena of every grade and kind. "All things flow" is the far-famed aphorism which sums up his philosophy. This eternal movement is not, however, formless, but is determined to ever-recurrent forms, and is obedient to law and rhythm.

He taught, then, that the eternal movement which constitutes existence is Fire. "This one order of all things (he affirms) was created by none of the gods, nor yet by any of mankind; but it was ever, and is, and shall be, eternal fire-ignited by measure and extinguished by measure." But more—he held that this Fire-motion is alive. It will be remembered that Thales had placed the cause of motion in matter itself, not in something other than matter; that is to say, he was to all

Heracleitus and the Cosmic Fire

intents and purposes a hylozoist. Heracleitus went a step farther, and maintained that the life in Fire-motion is *organic*, like to that which is manifested in the plant and animal worlds. His idea of the essential kinship of all things is very clear and complete.

He conceived, therefore, that soul is in no way fundamentally distinct from any other of the transformations of the ever-living Fire. And thus the problem which so grievously torments modern psychologists, that of the connection between soul and body, did not exist for him. And a notable corollary of his view is this. Since man has essential kinship with his environment, he can apprehend both the outer surface of things and their inner law; and it is in this recognition of their inner law that his true nature is to be found. Now if it be granted that this inner law can be apprehended by intuition as well as by conscious reasoning process, the corollary is one to which the nature-mystic can heartily subscribe. In fact, he recognises in it a statement of his own master principle.

The soul, as fire, depends on the cosmic Fire for sustenance, the breath being the physical medium ; and in this regard, all that was said of Anaximenes and " Breath," or Air, will have its place. But Heracleitus has a further thought which is in full harmony with the nature-mystic's chief contention. He holds that *sense perception* is also a medium, for the outer fire is thereby absorbed by the inner fire. The value of this thought remains in spite of the sage's doctrine of the body. For though the

Nature Mysticism

body is regarded by him as a clog on the activity of the inner fire, because it consists of water and earth (two forms in which the movement of the Fire is greatly reduced) it is nevertheless akin to the soul, and is itself destined, in the course of ceaseless change, to become Fire in its most living and active form.

Such is the central doctrine of this noted thinker, round which all his other teaching turned. Let us now ask, as in the corresponding cases of Thales and Anaximander, why the particular element was chosen as the Ground of all things. The answer to this question will furnish, as in the previous cases, much matter for our special purpose, since the emphasis will lie rather on the physical properties and functions of fire, than on its more abstract ontology.

It is obvious that Heracleitus would start with a knowledge of the speculations of his more immediate predecessors, and of the data on which they were based—the phenomena of circulation in nature, evaporation, mist, rain, melting, freezing, and the rest. And we find that in this direction he merely amplified the older systems, taking fire, instead of water or air, as his *Welt-stoff*. He also observed, with special care, certain suggestive cases of rarefaction by heat and condensation by cold ; as also the facts of constant decomposition and renewal in the vegetable and animal worlds. But the phenomenon which stands out as the chiefest determinant of his thought is one which

Heracleitus and the Cosmic Fire

is always bound to act as a powerful stimulant on a thoughtful mind—that of combustion.

The flame of an ordinary fire can still be a thing of wonder to the man whose mind is open to receive impressions even from the commonplace. How illusive it is !—dancing, darting, flickering, flashing —appearing, disappearing—unsubstantial yet active and almost miraculously potent. The effect upon the mind of primitive man must have been keen and vivid to the highest degree, and must have produced results of corresponding significance upon his spiritual development.

But the deeper kind of wonder is reserved for the systematic speculative thinker, whose attention is arrested by the phenomena of a steadily burning flame, say that of a lamp. The oil is sucked up into the wick and slowly decreases in volume. At the point where the flame begins it rises in vapour, becomes brilliant, and, in the case of a clear flame, disappears. There is thus a constant movement from below upwards. The flame has all the appearance of a " thing," with comparatively definite form and continued existence, and yet is never really the same, not for the minutest fraction of a moment. It is an appearance born of incessant motion—let the motion stop, the flame is gone. Where the burning is accompanied by smoke, there is an apparent return of volatilised matter to solid form.

Now let a philosopher like Heracleitus be meditating on nature as a circulatory system, and let

Nature Mysticism

him, by chance or otherwise, bring together in his mind the phenomena of a burning lamp and the cosmic facts for which he seeks an explanation— is it difficult to imagine his Eureka? At any rate, Heracleitus felt that in the phenomena of combustion he had gained an insight into the ultimate constitution of nature. And he concluded from them that there is no such thing as substance, properly so called, but simply constant movement; the movement *is* substance. The great solid-seeming cosmos is motion; some of it visible, some of it imperceptible; some of it rising upward to serve as fuel, some of it falling downward, after having fed the flame, to form the constituents of the present world. The motion is constant, the stream ever-flowing: no " thing " is ever at rest, and, if it were at rest, would disappear.

The marvel is that with such scanty data, Heracleitus was able to attain to views which are in truly remarkable harmony with the most advanced theories as to the constitution of matter. Nowadays the very qualities of hardness and impenetrability are being ascribed to motion—to the almost inconceivable rapidity of the whirling of electrons within the system of the atom. Le Bon, for example, in his "Evolution of Matter" and his "Evolution of Forces," contends that atoms are continually breaking down, radium presenting merely an extreme case of a general rule, and that the final product is something which is no longer matter. Robbed of motion, what we call matter

208

Heracleitus and the Cosmic Fire

disappears ! It eludes detection by any methods known to us, and ceases, therefore, so far as we are concerned, to be existent. Atoms, then, according to this modern doctrine, are complex systems of motion ; and bodies, all agree, are aggregates of atoms. It seems to follow that the ground of reality, from the point of view of physics, is motion. In short, as Heracleitus taught, the world is the result of ceaseless motion. Tyndall's doctrine of "heat as a mode of motion" is being generalised until it covers the whole field of material phenomena.

Or approach the theory of Heracleitus from the side of modern astronomy, the harmony between old and new is equally striking. All substances, said he, spring from fire and to fire they are bound to return. It does not require much special knowledge to realise that this statement contains the pith of the latest theories of the birth and death of worlds. From fire-mist, says the modern astronomer, they were condensed, and to fire-mist, by collisions or otherwise, they will return. What the particular stages may be, what the significance of the nebulæ, what the cosmic functions of electricity, and other like problems—may be, and will be, matter for keen debate. But the grand generalisation remains—from fire-mist back again to fire-mist.

How modern, also, the grand unity which such a theory gives to existence as a whole. Physics, psychology, sociology, even spiritual facts, all come under the sway of the vast generalisation, because all concerned with the same ultimate Reality. The

P 209

Nature Mysticism

most striking parallel is found, perhaps, in the doctrine of Energy, which is attracting so much attention at the present time, and of which Ostwald is a champion so doughty. It embodies an attempt to bring into one category the various physical forces together with the phenomena of organic evolution, of psychology, and of sociology in the largest sense. Whether the attempt is successful or not, it is a tribute to the genius of the ancient sage, though it seems to lack that definite element of consciousness, or soul-life, which was so adequately recognised by its great predecessor.

Many other points in the system of Heracleitus are worthy of the closest study. Intensely interesting, for example, is his doctrine that strife is the condition of harmony, and indeed of existence. Schelling reproduced this idea in his well-known theory of polarity; Hegel developed it in his dialectic triad—Thesis, Antithesis, Synthesis; and the electrical theories of matter and force now in vogue fall easily into line with it—not to speak of the dominant theory of evolution as involving a struggle for existence, and as applied in well-nigh all departments of enquiry and research. But it is enough to have grasped the central principle of Fire-motion to prove that the phenomena of fire have had an influence in the development of man's intellectual and spiritual life—an influence which cannot easily be exaggerated Heracleitus claims an honoured place in the lin of nature-mystics.

CHAPTER XXVIII

FIRE AND THE SUN

THERE can be no doubt, as already stated, that, of all physical phenomena, fire had the most marked effect upon the imagination of primitive man. He saw that it was utterly unlike anything else known to him, both in its properties and in its action. If of anything a divine nature could be predicated, it was fire—the standing miracle— at once destroying and life-giving—material and immaterial—pre-eminently an agent with strange and vast powers, known and unknown. For many objects and institutions a divine origin was sought; it could not fail to be the case with fire. Even the poor Tasmanian natives felt it could not be a thing of earth, and told each other how it was thrown down like a star by two black fellows who are now in the sky, the twin stars, Castor and Pollux. A great gap separates this simple tale from the elaborate Prometheus myth, and yet the same essential features appear in both: and between the two are found a varied series of stories and legends, belonging to many climes and ages, which ring the changes on the same funda-

211

Nature Mysticism

mental ideas. The whole of the ancient world believed that the origin of fire must be divine. And the various steps can be clearly traced by which the worship, originally accorded to the nature-power itself, was transferred to a spirit behind the power, and centred at last on the supreme Deity.

For primitive man, as Max Müller well points out, the phenomena of fire would present a dual aspect—on the one hand as a fatal and destructive element, on the other hand, as a beneficent and even homely agency. The lightning would be seen flashing from the one end of heaven to the other, darting down at times to set ablaze the forests and prairies, at times to maim and kill both animals and men. Thus experienced, it would strike terror into the beholders, and impress them with a vivid sense of the presence of spiritual powers. As a late product of the emotions and conceptions thus stimulated, we have the fine myth of the ancient nature goddess, Athene— sprung from the head of Zeus, the austere virgin, who was to become the personification of prudence, self-restraint, and culture, the celestial representative of the loftiest intellectual and spiritual ideals of the Greek world at its best. Hence, too, the group of conceptions which make the lightning and thunderbolts the weapons of the sky, putting them into the hands of the supreme ruler, and making them at last the symbols of law and order. " Out of the fire " (says Ezekiel) " went forth light-

212

Fire and the Sun

ning." " Out of the throne " (says the seer of the Apocalypse) " went forth lightnings."

In strong contrast is the beneficent aspect of fire, which, once known and " tamed," becomes almost a necessity for human life. It affords new protection against the cold, makes man peculiarly the cooking animal, and above all establishes the family hearth with all that is meant by " home." Of more distinctly utilitarian import are the uses of fire in fashioning tools and instruments, and the smelting of metals. And it is significant to note that man's use of fire almost certainly owed its origin to his emotional attitude towards it, culminating in worship. As many anthropologists have pointed out, the fire on the hearth had its unmistakable religious aspect, the result of the feeling of veneration for the " element " of fire before its production or use had been understood. And the kindling of the fire on the hearth was as much a sacrifice to the gods as a means to the cooking of food. Each house became a veritable temple of fire.

Wonderfully instructive, as well as fascinating it is to trace the development of the home idea as based on the emotional experiences stimulated by the mystic influences of fire. Each house, as was just stated, was regarded as a temple of the divine element; but the common house, the tribe house, was specially singled out for this honour, and became a temple properly so-called. When bands of citizens set out to found colonies in strange lands, they took with them glowing embers from the tribal or national hearth, as Æneas brought with him to Italy the sacred fire of Troy. Until lately, we are told, the German peasant just married would take to his new home a burning log from the family hearth.

The classical instance of the development of this idea is found in the cult of the Greek Hestia, the Latin Vesta, a goddess who was the personification of fire, the guardian of the household altar and of the welfare of cities and nations. She was worshipped fairly widely in Greece and Asia Minor, but principally in Rome, where a beautiful circular temple was dedicated to her service ; her ministers, the Vestal virgins, were held in the greatest honour and were chosen from among the loveliest and noblest of Roman maidens. In this temple was kept ever brightly burning the sacred fire supposed to have been kindled by the rays of the sun, and to have been brought by Æneas when he founded his kingdom in the new land of Italy. The extinction of this fire would have been regarded as the gravest public calamity, foreboding disaster. Its flames were intended to represent the *purity* of the goddess, thus emphasising the mystic aspect of another physical property of fire —its purifying power. "Our God" (said the writer of the Epistle to the Hebrews) "is a consuming fire."

Greece had its common hearth at Delphi. It was also supposed that at the centre of the earth

Fire and the Sun

there was a hearth which answered to that. In the Apocalypse we read of the altar with its sacred fire as central in heaven. Truly these concepts are persistent! And why? Because there is more than imagination in them; they are the products of ideas immanent in the material phenomena in which they are embodied, and through which they manifest themselves to the human soul.

There could not fail to be fire-gods many, and a study of their respective characters, especially in the earlier stages of their development, often furnishes a key to the intuitional workings of the primitive mind as prompted by the always arresting, and often terrorising phenomena of fire and flame. Max Müller's detailed study of the development of the Hindu god, Agni, was mentioned in an earlier chapter. The name originally means the Mover, and arose, doubtless, from the running, darting, leaping movement of flame. Beginning his career as a purely physical god, he advanced through various stages of spiritualisation until he became the supreme deity. Is not the problem of motion still one of the most fascinating and profound? Bergson's " L'Evolution créatrice " is one of the latest attempts to grapple with it, and those who in early India personified fire as the Mover were his legitimate predecessors.

The Greek Hephæstus personified the brightness of flame, and took shape as a god of ripe age, of muscular form, of serious countenance, but lame.

Nature Mysticism

Why lame ? Why this physical defect as a draw-
back to so much physical beauty and strength ?
A Frenchman, Emérie, suggests—" attendu la
marche inégale et vacillante de la flamme." Certainly fire, as compared with water and air, is
dependent on sustenance, as Heracleitus so well
realised, as also its consequent limitations in
regard to free and independent movement : but
the sage solved this difficulty by making the
Fire-motion feed, as it were, upon itself. The
god was represented as puny at birth because
flame, especially as kindled artificially, so often
starts from a tiny spark. His marriage to Aphrodite typifies " the association of fire with the life-
giving forces of nature." So, remarks Max Müller,
the Hindu Agni was the patron of marriage.
How many lines of thought open out before us
here, bringing us face to face, by pre-scientific
modes of mental activity, with some of the deepest
mysteries of human life !

Vulcan, the Latin parallel of Hephæstus, suggests to us the awe-inspiring phenomena of vol-
canoes, which, though not of frequent occurrence,
are calculated by virtue of their magnitude and
grandeur to stimulate emotion and intuition to an
exceptional degree. Fear would naturally pre-
dominate, but, even for the primitive mind, would
be one factor only in a complex whole. Matthew
Arnold has attempted to portray the soul-storm
raised by the sight of the molten crater of Ætna.
He makes Empedocles, the poet-philosopher, climb

216

Fire and the Sun

the summit of the mountain, gaze for the last time on the realm of nature spread around, and apostrophise the stars above and the volcanic fires beneath his feet.

> " And thou, fiery world,
> That sapp'st the vitals of this terrible mount
> Upon whose charred and quaking crust I stand—
> Thou, too, brimmest with life."

Note here again the sense of life—of kinship, so fundamental to Nature Mysticism. And so to the close.

> " And therefore, O ye elements ! I know—
> Ye know it too—it hath been granted me
> Not to die wholly, not to be all enslaved.
> I feel it in this hour. The numbing cloud
> Mounts off my soul ; I feel it, I breathe free,
> Is it but for a moment ?
> —Ah, boil up, ye vapours !
> Leap and roar, thou sea of fire !
> My soul glows to meet you.
> Ere it flag, ere the mists
> Of despondency and gloom
> Rush over it again,
> Receive me, save me !
>   [He plunges into the crater.]"

Out of the ancient beliefs and myths concerning subterranean fires grew up the enormously important beliefs in Hell and Purgatory, which attained such abnormal proportions in mediæval times, and which are by no means yet extinct. The most vivid picture of Hell, founded largely on ancient material, though with a Biblical basis,

217

Nature Mysticism

is found in Milton. In language which recalls the
Titanomachy, the poet tells of Satan and his
myrmidons hurled from heaven.

> "Him the almighty Power
> Hurled headlong flaming from th' ætherial sky,
> With hideous ruin and combustion, down
> To bottomless perdition, there to dwell
> In adamantine chains and penal fire."

Confounded for a time by his fall, he lies rolling
in the fiery gulf ; but at length, rolling round
his baleful eyes, he sees

> "A dungeon horrible, on all sides round,
> As one great furnace flamed ; yet from those flames
> No light, but rather darkness visible
> Served only to discover sights of woe,
> Regions of sorrow, doleful shades, where peace
> And rest can never dwell, hope never comes
> That comes to all ; but torture without end
> Still urges, and a fiery deluge fed
> With ever-burning sulphur unconsumed."

What manner of intuitions are embodied here ?
Perchance we are beginning to treat them too
lightly, as also the Hindu doctrine of Karma ;
for the universe, after all, is the scene of the reign
of law. But however this may be, we are glad to
emerge, with Dante, from the regions of punitive
flames into the regions of the fires that purge—
into the pure air that surrounds the Isle of Purgatory.

> "Sweet hue of eastern sapphire, that was spread
> O'er the serene aspect of the pure air,
> High up as the first circle, to mine eyes

218

Fire and the Sun

Unwonted joy renewed, soon as I 'scaped
Forth from the atmosphere of deadly gloom
That had mine eyes and bosom filled with grief."

Shall we invest with like purgatorial powers the
flaming swords that barred the way to Paradise ?
Is such the inner meaning of the appeal :

" do thou my tongue inspire
Who touched Isaiah's hallowed lips with fire " ?

The more hostile aspects of fire are most strikingly embodied in the Teutonic giant Logi (Flame)
with his children, who were supposed to be the
authors of every great conflagration, and who
might be seen in the midst of the flames, their
heads crowned with chaplets of fire. They may be
taken, like the Greek giants and Titans, as personifications of the wild brute forces of nature, which
strive to hinder man's work and destroy what he
has made. For, as Schiller says :

" the elements are hostile
To the work of human hand."

For such are but some out of the many forms in
which man has struggled to give expression to
his intuitions that there is something wrong in
nature—to his deep sense of division and conflict
in the cosmic process. Heracleitus, as we saw,
held that conflict is an essential condition of
existence. At any rate, it is true, that order is
only won by severe conflict with destructive and
irregular powers. An ancient expression of this

219

experience is found in the long contest waged between Zeus and the other children of Cronos. A modern expression is found in Huxley's illustration of the fenced garden that, if untended, speedily returns to its wild condition. In the framing and moulding of this experience, the hostile aspects of fire have played no insignificant part.

In this context it would be natural to treat of the Sun as the predominant manifestation of fire, of which Shelley, in his hymn to Apollo, has said :

> " I am the eye with which the Universe
> Beholds itself and knows itself divine."

The various sun-gods would be passed in review, Ra of the Egyptians, Apollo of the Greeks, and the various forms of sun-worship, from the most primitive times down through the Persian religion, that of the Peruvians, the " children of the sun," to that of the modern Parsees—and that of the unnamed multitudes who in substance have echoed the words which Moore puts into the mouths of the Hyperboreans :

> " To the Sun-god all our hearts and lyres
>   By day, by night belong ;
> And the breath we draw from his living fires
>   We give him back in song."

But the subject is too great and is deserving of special treatment. Certain of the more essential conceptions involved will come before us in the chapter on light. Mirabeau on his death-bed would seem to have put the whole matter in the

Fire and the Sun

briefest space—" Si ce n'est pas là Dieu, c'est du
moins son cousin-german." Turner, on his death-
bed, was briefer and bolder still—" The sun is
God." Knowing the man and knowing his work,
we can understand what he meant. Put it the
other way round, we have the same, and yet the
fuller truth—" the Lord God is a Sun."

CHAPTER XXIX

LIGHT AND DARKNESS

ROBERT FLUDD, the English Rosicrucian, who died in 1637, wrote a treatise on the universe, in which he taught that man was a microcosm of the macrocosm, and that light and darkness are the two great principles of existence, the one of animate, the other of inanimate nature. He held that soul and life are every day shed from the sun upon all objects open to his beams. For such doctrines as these he was denounced as practically an atheist! Fortunately the times have changed, though we have still much to learn in the way of rational tolerance and sympathetic receptivity.

Who shall say how old is this idea of two distinct, and generally opposing principles, the light and the dark? The Babylonian cosmology carries us a long way back, but not to the beginning of such mystical conceptions. For in that cosmology Marduk is a well-developed god of light, with Tiâmat as his antithesis, the goddess of the dark, and the nature and course of the deadly contest between them has taken form in a well-defined series of myths.

Light and Darkness

One of the most obvious emotional effects of darkness is to inspire fear, and there are few who have not in some degree and on some occasions experienced a sense of discomfort in the dark—a chill, or a shrinking, which in certain cases, especially with children, may amount to terror. It is possible that we have here, as is often contended, an organic reminiscence of the experience of our remote ancestors. Certainly it is not difficult for us to sympathise with the primitive dread of darkness, nor to understand the transition to the conception of darkness as a hostile power. But there is also an element which may be regarded as simply personal and individual—a natural anticipation of unknown dangers, and a sense of helplessness should the apprehensions be realised. There is, moreover, an element of a still more directly mystical character, that which Everett describes as a feeling that in the darkness the familiar world is swept away and that we are touching the limits of the natural. Hence the chill of the unknown and supernatural.

However this may be, the fact remains that from the earliest known times, there have been powers of darkness set over against the powers of light ; and the conflict between them has suggested with exceptional vividness the conflict between good and evil. The opening verses of the Bible, with their chaos and darkness, and the sublime command—" Let there be light "—are in line with a vast body of primitive myth and speculation

223

which represents the good God as the Creator of light, or as light itself over against the dark. The mysticism of the prologue to St. John's Gospel both represented and fostered ideas which were current in the earliest Christian communities and have coloured the whole of the primitive Christian literature.

So in the most ancient of the classical mythologies, Night was one of the oldest deities, daughter of Chaos, and sister of Erebus, the dark underworld. So in Persian dogmatic we have the same essential concepts. From the beginning existed uncreated light and uncreated darkness—the opposing kingdoms of Ahura and Ahriman.

Who shall say what great cosmic facts lie behind these vague and looming intuitions ? The physical merges by insensible degrees into the æsthetic, the moral, the spiritual. On the one hand, the chill, the blankness, the negation, sometimes the horror, of the darkness. And on the other hand the purity and beauty, the colour and effulgence of the light —above all, its joy-giving, life-giving, though noiseless, energy.

Coming down to the present, we ask if these mystic influences of light and of darkness still retain their power. Can we doubt it ? We have Milton's Melancholy, " of Cerberus and blackest Midnight born "—" where brooding darkness spreads his jealous wings." All this no mere refurbishing of classical lore, but the outcome of deep sympathy with the poets of the prime. And the same is true

Light and Darkness

of his buoyant lines that describe the breaking of
the day, when morn

> " Waked by the circling hours, with rosy hand
> Unbarr'd the gates of light."

In sympathy, too, with the old belief in Ahura's final
victory is Emerson's declaration that " the night is
for the day, but the day is not for the night."

Browning finely discriminates the grades of
darkness in Sordello, where he addresses Dante as

> " pacer of the shore
> Where glutted hell disgorgeth filthiest gloom,
> Unbitten by its whirring sulphur-spume ;
> Or whence the grieved and obscure waters slope
> Into a darkness quieted by hope ;
> Plucker of amaranths grown beneath God's eye
> In gracious twilights where His chosen lie."

Homer and Job are at one in associating darkness with the grave, and all that the grave implies.
" Before I go whence I shall not return, even to the
land of darkness and the shadow of death." Homer
and Ecclesiastes are one in love of the sunlit sky :
" Truly the light is sweet, and a pleasant thing it
is for the eyes to behold the sun." And Shakespeare in fullest sympathy cries :

> " See how the sun
> Walks o'er the top of yonder eastern hill."

And sunrises and sunsets wake in Wordsworth's
soul the thought of

> " The light that never was on sea or land."

Q   225

Nature Mysticism

And it is the world-old feeling of life and joy that breathes in Blake's lines "To Morning":

> "O holy virgin! clad in purest white,
> Unlock heaven's golden gates and issue forth;
> Awake the dawn that sleeps in heaven; let light
> Rise from the chambers of the east, and bring
> The honey'd dew that cometh on waking day.
> O radiant morning, salute the sun,
> Roused like a huntsman to the chase, and with
> Thy buskin'd feet appear upon our hills."

But what of modern science? Does not that eliminate the mystic element? Far from that, it increases it. The dominant theory is that light is a sensation caused by waves in ether which travel at a speed of 186,000 miles a second. Of this theory Whewell wrote in 1857 that Optics had "reached her grand generalisation in a few years by sagacious and happy speculations." But it was not thus that a halting-place was gained. For there succeeded the discoveries of Faraday, Clerk Maxwell, Hertz, and other great physicists who used the old theory merely as a foundation for a superstructure of unsuspected and wondrous proportions. The theory of electrons came to the front, and the phenomena of light are being linked on to those of electricity. The phenomena of electricity, again, are being linked on to those of life. And thus, as ever where our deepest intuitions are concerned, the nature-mystic finds himself in harmony with and abreast of the latest developments of modern knowledge.

226

Light and Darkness

At the dawn of human thought light and life were dimly but persistently felt to be akin, if not identical. And now we know it was a deep prompting of mother nature which caused men to give to their divine beings the simple name—" the Bright Ones."

CHAPTER XXX

THE EXPANSE OF HEAVEN—COLOUR

"The broad open eye of the solitary sky."

CHARLES LAMB, with his native sensitiveness, considered this line to be too terrible for art. Its suggestion of " the irresponsive blankness of the universe " was for him too naked and poignant. And yet, in certain of his aspects, nature is undoubtedly irresponsive to man—aloof from his affairs—more especially in her pageantry of the heavens, the sun, the moon and the stars. But this feeling of aloofness is not constant, nor even normal, as witness the exquisite lines in Peter Bell :

" At noon, when by the forest's edge
He lay beneath the branches high,
The soft blue sky did never melt
Into his heart—he never felt
The witchery of the soft blue sky ! "

Whether in its friendly or its alien aspects, the widespread, all-embracing arch of the heavens has, in all times and climes, profoundly influenced human thought, more particularly so in lands where the sky is clear and bright and the horizons extended. Its effect, in flat and desert regions, on

228

The Expanse of Heaven—Colour

the development of monotheistic beliefs was noted
in an early chapter. In India it has played the
chiefest part in fostering abstract universalism
and the conception of a pantheistic Absolute, and
has tempted men to views which leave no room for
human initiative nor for belief in objective reality.
And when we recognise the wide and deep influence
exerted by Buddhism upon ethics and metaphysics,
ancient and modern, we realise that the dome of
heaven has proved itself a mystic force of the first
rank.

We must be on our guard, however, lest we exaggerate this pantheistic or universalistic influence.
We have a sufficient corrective in the development
of Dyaus, an ancient god of the sky, who became,
in one of his later forms, the Greek Zeus—that is
to say, a king of gods as well as of men—the ruler
of Olympus—the supreme member of a polytheistic
community. And this development is but representative of a large class which have proceeded on
similar lines—the class which come to their own
in the concept of a Heaven-Father. For example,
Tylor shows that, in the religion of the North American Indians, " the Heaven-god displays perfectly
the gradual blending of the material sky itself with
its personal deity "; and that the Chinese Tien,
Heaven, the highest deity of the state religion, un-
derwent a like theologic development. The mystic
influence remains in Christianity, as witness Keble:

> " The glorious sky embracing all
> Is like the Maker's love."

229

Nature Mysticism

It may be affirmed, then, without fear of contradiction, that the elemental phenomena of the sky, overarching all with its unlimited span, has provided men with the idea of an all-embracing deity —this idea, among others, is immanent there and awaits still further development.

Awaits further development—for the mystic influences persist and suggest deeper interpretations. Browning, though not an avowed nature-mystic, felt the thrill and the emotion of the sky.

> " The morn has enterprise, deep quiet droops
> With evening, triumph takes the sunset hour."

As for the emotional value of the universal span of the sky, its power to tranquillise by a sense of vast harmony and unity, Christina Rossetti knew it :

> " Heaven o'erarches you and me,
>   And all earth's gardens and her graves.
> Look up with me, until we see
> The day break and the shadows flee.
> What though to-night wrecks you and me
>   If so to-morrow saves ? "

Here, as is almost inevitable, the thought of the expanse is associated with the alternate coming on of darkness and the breaking of the dawn ; but the change and alternation gains its unity and ultimate significance from the all-inclusiveness of the sky as the abiding element.

Walt Whitman brings out another aspect of this subtle but powerful influence. He addresses the sky : " Hast Thou, pellucid, in Thy azure depths, medicine for case like mine ? (Ah, the physical shatter and troubled spirit of me the last three years.) And dost Thou subtly, mystically now drip it through the air invisibly upon me ? "

In similar mood Jefferies writes : " I turned to the blue heaven over, gazing into its depth, inhaling its exquisite colour and sweetness. The rich blue of the unattainable flower of the sky drew my soul towards it, and there it rested, for pure colour is rest of heart."

And thus " the witchery of the soft blue sky " launches us naturally into the subject of the sky as colour ; and not of blue only, but of that vast range of hues and gradations which display their beauty and their glory in the four quarters of heaven during each move onwards of the earth from sunrise to sunrise. Tennyson's description is vivid and splendid. The shipwrecked Enoch Arden is waiting for a sail, and sees

" Every day
Tho sunrise broken into scarlet shafts
Among the palms and ferns and precipices ;
The blaze upon the waters to the east ;
The blaze upon his island overhead ;
The blaze upon tho waters to the west ;
Then tho great stars that globed themselves in Heaven,
The hollower-bellowing ocean, and again
The scarlet shafts of sunrise."

But of special interest here is the fact that the blue of the vault is never mentioned—only the scarlet shafts of sunrise and the blaze. Whether this omission was intentional or not, may be uncertain.

Nature Mysticism

But it brings to mind the strange fact that the perception and naming of this blue are comparatively recent acquirements. In the old hymns of the Rigveda the chariot of the sun is described as glowing with varied colour, and its horses as gold-like or beaming with sevenfold hues; but although there was a word for the blue of the sea and for indigo dye, this word is never applied to the brightness of the sunlit vault. So, still more strangely, we find that notwithstanding the laughing blue of the Greek sky, old Homer never calls it blue! He has his rosy-fingered dawn, the parallel of Tennyson's scarlet shafts; but the daylight sky seems to have been for him as for Enoch Arden, a "blaze." Nor is the omission supplied in the later classical literature; and the older Greek writers on science use such epithets as "air-coloured," as substitutes for more specific terms. A German scholar who has examined the ancient writings of the Chinese claims for them priority in the recognition of the blue of the sky, and points out that in the Schi-king, a collection of songs from about 1709 to 618 B.C., the sky is called the vaulted blue, as in the more modern language it is called the reigning blue.

Delitzsch, from whom much of what is just stated has been derived (as also from Gladstone's paper on Homer's colour-sense) does not find the blue of the sky recognised in Europe earlier than the oldest Latin poets of the third century B.C., who use *caerulus* of the sky, and henceforth this

The Expanse of Heaven—Colour

epithet takes its place in literature, Pagan and Christian. And the appreciation of the heaven-colour develops apace until we have Wordsworth's " Witchery of the soft blue sky."

The explanation of this late development is a problem of much interest from the point of view of the physiologist and the psychologist, in its bearing on the history of the special senses. It would not be safe to say that the colour was not perceived, in a somewhat loose sense of that term, but rather that it was not consciously distinguished. As with the child, so with primitive man, the strong sensations are the first to be definitely apprehended —the glow of flame, the scarlet and crimson of dawn and sunset, the gold of the sun and moon and stars. Red and yellow were the first to assert themselves ; and the two are significantly combined in Homer's descriptions of the dawn—the yellow of the crocus as a garment, and the flush of the rose for the fingered rays.

We must not imagine, however, that the failure to distinguish the hues and grades of blue argued any lack of appreciation of the quality of pure, translucent depth which characterises the clear sunlit sky. A striking proof to the contrary is found in a description in the book of Exodus, where a vision of God is described, and where we read that " under His feet was as it were a work of transparent sapphire, and as it were the body of heaven in its clearness." We recall also the exquisite expression, " the clear shining after rain."

233

Nature Mysticism

The nature-mystic, therefore, need not eliminate the blue of the vault, the brightness of the sky, as an influence in moulding man's spiritual nature in the early days. It remains true, however, that the delicate discrimination of colour is a comparatively recent acquirement, and that thus the modern world has gained a new wealth of phenomena in the sphere of direct sensation. And this recently acquired subtlety of colour-sense is bound to bring with it a corresponding wealth of mystical intuition. The older attempts at colour symbolism point the way—the red of blood, the crimson of flame, the white of the lily, the blush of the rose, the gleam of steel or silver, the glow of gold, the green of the mantle worn by mother-earth, all these, and numberless others have played their part as subtle mystic influences. But there is more and better yet to come. Milton could write:

> "O welcome pure-eyed Faith, white-handed Hope,
>   Thou hovering angel, girt with golden wings!"

As tints, so significances, more delicate shall be won by man's soul in contact with nature. For colour is as varied as love. "Colour" (says Ruskin) "is the type of love. Hence it is especially connected with the blossoming of the earth, and with its fruits; also with the spring and fall of the leaf, and with the morning and evening of the day, in order to show the waiting of love about the birth and death of man."

234

CHAPTER XXXI

THE MOON—A SPECIAL PROBLEM

THE contention of the nature-mystic is that man can enter into direct communion with the objects in his physical environment, inasmuch as they are akin to himself in their essential nature. Now Goethe says :

> " The stars excite no craving,
> One is happy simply in their glory."

And Schopenhauer asks why the sight of the full moon has upon us an influence so soothing and elevating. His explanation is in harmony with the general trend of his philosophical doctrine. He says that the moon has so little relation to our personal concerns that it is not an object of willing. We are content to contemplate her in passive receptivity. We have here a problem which is well worthy of discussion. Let us bring the matter to the test of actual experience as embodied in modern prose and poetry. For while it goes without saying that the qualities of physical remoteness, elevation, and vastness, have their own peculiar mystical power, and that they are especially manifested in the phenomena of the starry heaven, there is a

235

Nature Mysticism

danger of emphasising this fact to the detriment of the basic principle of Nature Mysticism. In order to bring the discussion within reasonable limits, let it be confined to Schopenhauer's example :

> " That orbéd maiden, with white fire laden,
>   Whom mortals call the moon."

Is it true that there is, alongside of the feeling of her remoteness, none of the active emotion which essential kinship would lead us to anticipate ?

Appeal might at once be made to the proverbial " crying for the moon " ; and there would be more in the appeal than might appear at first sight. For there comes at once into mind the sublimination of this longing in the lovely myth of Endymion which so powerfully affected Keats, and fascinated even Browning. Appeal might also be made to the sweet naturalism of St. Francis with his endearing name, " Our sister, the Moon."

There is, moreover, the enormous mass of magical and superstitious lore which gives the moon a very practical and direct influence over human affairs. This may be ruled out as not based on facts ; but it remains as an evidence of a sense of kinship of a practical kind. And if this fails, there is the teaching of modern science. We now know that the tides are evidence of the moon's never-ceasing interposition in terrestrial affairs, and that, apart from her functions as a light-giver, innumerable human happenings are dependent on her motion and position. There is

236

The Moon—A Special Problem

even a theory that she is part and parcel of the earth itself, having been torn out of the bed of the Pacific. And, in any case, her surface has been explored, so far as it is turned to us, and, with a marvellous accuracy of detail, mapped out, and named. Science, then, while measuring her distance, certainly does not increase the sense of our alienation from her.

But let us turn, as proposed, to the writings of modern seers and interpreters. See how Keats associates the moon with the humblest and most homely things of earth :

> " Some shape of beauty moves away the pall
>   From our dark spirits. Such the sun, the moon,
>   Trees old and young, sprouting a shady boon
>   For simple sheep ; and such are daffodils
>   With the green world they live in."

There is no sense of a gap here, in passing from heaven to earth. In a strain of stronger emotion, he makes Endymion speak :

> " Lo ! from opening clouds, I saw emerge
>   The loveliest moon that ever silvered o'er
>   A shell from Neptune's goblet ; she did soar
>   So passionately bright, my dazzled soul
>   Commingling with her argent spheres did roll
>   Through clear and cloudy."

There is little of Schopenhauer's passive and contemplative receptivity here ! Rather a mingling of being in a sweep through space.

Catullus sang how that :

Nature Mysticism

> " Near the Delian olive-tree
> Latonia gave thy life to thee
> That thou shouldst be for ever queen
> Of mountains and of forests green ;
> Of every deep glen's mystery ;
> Of all streams in their melody."

And Wordsworth, in fullest sympathy enforces the old-world imaginings. He dwells on the homely aspect :

> " Wanderer ! that stoop'st so low, and com'st so near
> To human life's unsettled atmosphere ;
> Who lov'st with Night and Silence to partake,
> So might it seem, the cares of them that wake ;
> And through the cottage-lattice softly peeping,
> Dost shield from harm the humblest of the sleeping "—

And links on these friendly thoughts to the mythical spirit of the past :

> " well might that fair face
> And all those attributes of modest grace,
> In days when Fancy wrought unchecked by fear,
> Down to the green fields fetch thee from thy sphere,
> To sit in leafy woods by fountains clear."

Or take the famous Homeric simile so finely translated by Tennyson :

> " As when in Heaven the stars above the moon
> Look beautiful, when all the winds are laid,
> And every height comes out, and jutting peak
> And valley, and the immeasurable heavens
> Break open to their highest, and all the stars
> Shine, and the shepherd gladdens in his heart."

The stars are here associated with the moon—so much the better for the principle now defended.

238

The Moon—A Special Problem

Compare this with some lines from Goethe himself —the Goethe who would persuade us that the stars excite no craving, and that we are happy simply in their glory. He thus addresses the Moon :

" Bush and vale thou fill'st again
    With thy misty ray
And my spirit's heavy chain
    Castest far away.
Thou dost o'er my fields extend
    Thy sweet soothing eye,
Watching, like a gentle friend,
    O'er my destiny."

Browning felt the charm of a lambent moon :

" Voluptuous transport rises with the corn
    Beneath a warm moon like a happy face."

So with an English picture from Kirke White :

" Moon of harvest, herald mild
    Of plenty, rustic labour's child,
    Hail ! O hail ! I greet thy beam,
    As soft it trembles o'er the stream,
    And gilds the straw-thatched hamlet wide,
    Where Innocence and Peace reside ;
'Tis thou that gladd'st with joy the rustic throng,
Promptest the tripping dance, th' exhilarating song."

To emphasise this aspect is not to forget that there is another. Wordsworth experienced both types of emotion. Time, he sings :

" that frowns
In her destructive flight on earthly crowns,
Spares thy cold splendour ; still those far-shot beams
Tremble on dancing waves and rippling streams
With stainless touch, as chaste as when thy praise
Was sung by Virgin-choirs in festal lays."

Nature Mysticism

But abundant evidence is available to prove that the position taken by Goethe and Schopenhauer may easily lead to a loss of true perspective. The moon and stars, though remote, are also near: though they start trains of passive and contemplative thought, they also stimulate active emotions and even passionate yearnings. What more passionate than Shelley ?

> " The desire of the moth for the star,
>   Of the night for the morrow,
> The devotion to something afar
>   From the sphere of our sorrow."

There do not seem to be many poets who have brought into clear antithesis and relief this dual aspect of the mystic influence of the heavenly bodies. But it definitely arrested the imagination and thought of Clough, whose poem, "Selene," deals wholly with this theme. It is too long for quotation here, though the whole of it would be admirably in place. Enough is given to show its general drift. The Earth addresses the Moon :

> " My beloved, is it nothing
> Though we meet not, neither can,
> That I see thee, and thou me,
> That we see and see we see,
> When I see I also feel thee ;
> Is it nothing, my beloved ?
>
> .   .   .   .   .   .
>
> O cruel, cruel lot, still thou rollest, stayest not,
> Lookest onward, look'st before,
> Yet I follow evermore.
>
> .   .   .   .   .   .

240

The Moon—A Special Problem

Cruel, cruel, didst thou only
Feel as I feel evermore,
A force, though in, not of me,
Drawing inward, in, in, in,
Yea, thou shalt though, ere all endeth,
Thou shalt feel me closer, closer,
My beloved!

.   .   .   .   .   .

The inevitable motion
Bears us both upon its line
Together, you as me,
Together and asunder,
Evermore. It so must be."

It behoves the nature-mystic, then, to be whole-hearted in defence of his master principle. *Homo sum, et humani a me nil alienum puto*—so said Terence. The nature-mystic adopts and expands his dictum. He substitutes *mundani* for *humani*, and includes in his *mundus*, as did the Latins, and as did the Greeks in their *cosmos*, not only the things of earth but the expanse of heaven.

CHAPTER XXXII

EARTH, MOUNTAINS, AND PLAINS

And thus the three great nature-philosophers of the old world, Thales, Anaximenes, and Heraclitus, have been our guides, so to speak, in surveying the most striking phenomena of water, air, and fire. The fourth member of the ancient group of " elements " has received but incidental treatment. Obviously it could hardly be otherwise, especially within the limits which such a study as this imposes. The varied and wondrous forms of vegetable and animal life have likewise made but brief and transient appearances ; but this omission has been due to a definite intention expressed at the outset. It may nevertheless be well, before concluding, to cast a glance over the rich provinces which still lie open to the nature-mystic for further discovery and research.

The more striking features of the landscape have always arrested attention and stimulated the mystic sense. The peculiar influence of heights has been noted at an earlier stage, though but cursorily. Much might be said of the enormous effect of mountain scenery. The most direct form of nature-feeling finds expression in Scott and

Earth, Mountains, and Plains

Byron ; and the description of crags, ravines, peaks and gorges, bulks largely in their writings. Typical are these lines from " Manfred " :

> " Ye crags upon whose extreme edge
> I stand, and on the torrent's brink beneath
> Behold the tall pines dwindled as to shrubs
> In dizziness of distance."

or Shelley with his

> " Eagle-baffling mountain
> Black, wintry, dead, unmeasured, without herb,
> Insect, or beast, or shape, or sound of life."

Indeed there are few poets, even those who are chiefly concerned with man and his doings, who do not often turn to mountain scenery at least for similes. And it could not be otherwise ; for the immanent ideas here manifested are self-assertive in character and specially rich in number and variety. As it has been well expressed, nature's pulse here seems to beat more quickly. In olden days the high places of the earth associated themselves with myths of gods and Titans. Fully representative of the world of to-day, Tennyson asks :

> " Hast thou no voice, O Peak,
> That standest high above all ? "

And his answer turns on the mystic bonds that bind the deep and the height into a cycle of interdependent activities.

> " The deep has power on the height,
> And the height has power on the deep.

.   .   .   .   .   .

243

Nature Mysticism

A deep below the deep
  And a height beyond the height !
Our hearing is not hearing,
  And our seeing is not sight."

Or Morris gives the mysticism a more personal turn :

" Oh, snows so pure ! oh, peaks so high !
I lift to you a hopeless eye,
I see your icy ramparts drawn
Between the sleepers and the dawn ;
I see you when the sun has set
Flush with the dying daylight yet.

.   .   .   .   .   .

Oh, snows so pure ! oh, peaks so high !
I shall not reach you till I die."

And now that modern geology is revealing to us more and more of the origin and structure of the mountain ranges of the world, and telling us more and more of the wondrous materials which go to their building, the field for mysticism is being widely extended.

Different, but hardly less powerful, is the influence of hill scenery—whether they

" in the distance lie
Blue and yielding as the sky,"

or whether their gentle slopes are climbed and their delicate beauties seen close at hand. As Ruskin has averred, even the simplest rise can suggest the mountain ; but it also has a mystic charm of its own, complementary to that of the sheltered vale, which is exquisite alike in its

244

natural simplicity, and in its response to the labours of man, where some

> " kneeling hamlet drains
> The chalice of the grapes of God."

But though the influence of mountains, hills, ravines, and vales, is obvious even to the superficial enquirer, it should not obscure for us the very real, if less potent influence of lowlands, plains, and deserts. More especially subtle in its effect upon the spirit of man, is the loneliness of wildernesses, the prairies, the pampas, the tundras, the Saharas. The Greek Pan was essentially a god of the wild, unploughed surfaces of the earth. Hence, also, the frequent conjunction of the wilderness and silent meditation and ascetic discipline. Schopenhauer suggests that one secret of the spell of mountain scenery is the permanence of the sky-line. Shall we say that one secret of the solitary place is the turning in of the human spirit upon itself because of the sameness of the permanent sky-line?

The effect of scenery upon religion was treated of in illustration of the general principle of Nature Mysticism—the kinship of man and his physical environment. No less marked has been the effect of scenery upon art. The theme is now somewhat well worn, but its true significance is seldom apprehended. For if art is concerned with the realm of the ideal, or rather, perhaps, with the real in its more ideal aspects, then it follows that

245

whatever has an influence on art has an influence on the spiritual development of the people among whom any particular mode or school of art may establish itself. An interesting phase of such influence is found in Geikie's suggestion as to the presence of the humorous element in the myths and legends of northern Europe. " The grotesque contours" (he says) " of many craggy slopes where, in the upstanding pinnacles of naked rock, an active imagination sees forms of men and of animals in endless whimsical repetitions, may sometimes have suggested the particular form of the ludicrous which appears in the popular legend. But the natural instinct of humour which saw physical features in a comic light, and threw a playful human interest over the whole face of nature, was a distinctively Teutonic character-istic." There opens out here an unexplored region for original research. Taking the nature-mystic's mode of experience as a basis for enquiry, how far is the comic a purely subjective affair, con-cerned only, as Bergson contends, with man, and only found in external phenomena by virtue of their reflecting his affairs ; or how far has it a place of its own in the universe at large ?

To conclude this slight sketch of the Nature Mysticism of the solid earth, let us bring together an ancient and a recent expression of the emotion these purely terrestrial phenomena can arouse. There is one of the Homeric hymns which is ad-dressed to " the Earth, Mother of All." Its begin-

Earth, Mountains, and Plains

ning and its ending are as follows (in Shelley's translation) :

> " O universal mother, who dost keep
> From everlasting thy foundations deep,
> Eldest of things, Great Earth, I sing of thee.
>
> .   .   .   .   .
>
> Mother of gods, thou wife of starry Heaven,
> Farewell ! be thou propitious."

Is there not a living continuity between the emotional element in that grand old hymn and the strong full modern sentiment in this concluding stanza of Brown's " Alma Mater " ?

> " O mother Earth, by the bright sky above thee,
> I love thee, O, I love thee !
> So let me leave thee never,
> But cling to thee for ever,
> And hover round thy mountains,
> And flutter round thy fountains,
>   And pry into thy roses fresh and red ;
> And blush in all thy blushes,
> And flush in all thy flushes,
> And watch when thou art sleeping,
> And weep when thou art weeping,
> And be carried with thy motion,
> As the rivers and the ocean,
> As the great rocks and the trees are—
> O mother, this were glorious life,
>   This were not to be dead.
> O mother Earth, by the bright sky above thee,
> I love thee, O, I love thee ! "

CHAPTER XXXIII

SEASONS, VEGETATION, ANIMALS

THE seasons and the months, especially those of the temperate zones—how saturated with mysticism! The wealth of illustration is so abounding that choice is wellnigh paralysed. Poets and nature lovers are never weary of drawing on its inexhaustible supplies. Take these verses from Tennyson's " Early Spring " :

> " Opens a door in Heaven ;
>   From skies of glass
> A Jacob's ladder falls
>   On greening grass,
> And o'er the mountain-walls
>   Young angels pass.
>
> For now the Heavenly Power
>   Makes all things new
> And thaws the cold and fills
>   The flower with dew ;
> The blackbirds have their wills,
>   The poets too."

Or take these exultant lines from Coventry Patmore's " Revulsion " Canto :

> " 'Twas when the spousal time of May
>   Hangs all the hedge with bridal wreaths,

Seasons, Vegetation, Animals

And air's so sweet the bosom gay
   Gives thanks for every breath it breathes ;
When like to like is gladly moved,
   And each thing joins in Spring's refrain,
' Let those love now who never loved ;
   Let those who have loved, love again.' "

Recall the poems that celebrate in endless chorus the emotions stirred by the pomp and glory of the summer ; by the fruitfulness or sadness of the mellow autumn ; by the keen exhilaration or the frozen grip of winter. Some poets, like Blake, have written special odes or sonnets on all the four ; some like Keats, in his " Ode to Autumn," have lavished their most consummate art on the season which most appealed to them. Each month, too, has its bards ; its special group of qualities and the sentiments they stimulate. Truly the heart of the nature-mystic rejoices as he reflects on the inexhaustibility of material and of significance here presented !

And what of the flowers ? Once again the theme is inexhaustible. The poets vie with one another in their efforts to give to even the humblest flowers their emotional and mystic setting. Some of the loveliest of the old-world myths are busied with accounting for the form or colour of the flowers. Wordsworth's Daffodils, Burns's Daisy, Tennyson's " Flower in the Crannied Wall," these are but fair blooms in a full and dazzling cluster. Flowers (said a certain divine) are the sweetest things God ever made and forgot

Nature Mysticism

to put a soul into. The nature-mystic thankfully acknowledges the sweetness, but he questions the absence of the soul! The degree of individuality is matter for grave debate; but to assume its absence is to place oneself out of focus for gaining true and living insight into nature's being. How much more deep-founded is Wordsworth's faith "that every flower enjoys the air it breathes."

Let us bring this matter to the test in regard to the big brothers of the flowers—the trees. Passing by the ample range of striking and beautiful myths and legends (packed as many of them are with mystic meaning), let us turn to the expressions of personal feeling which the literature of various ages provides in abundance—limiting the view to certain typical examples. The Teutonic myth of the World-tree was dealt with fully in the chapter on Subterranean Waters. But it is well to mention it now in connection with the far-extended group of myths which centre in the idea of a tree of life, which preserved their vitality in changing forms, and which even appear in Dante in his account of the mystical marriage under the withered tree. Virgil was a lover of trees; the glade and the forest appealed to him by the same magic of suggested life as that which works on the modern poet or nature-lover.

It is generally supposed that, in England, the loving insight of the nature-mystic was practically unknown until Collins, Thomson, and Crabbe led the way for the triumph of the Lake poets.

Seasons, Vegetation, Animals

This may be true for many natural objects—but it is not true for all. How fresh these lines from an address to his muse by Wither:

> " By the murmur of a spring,
>   Or the least bough's rustolling ;
>   By a daisy whose leaves spread,
>   Shut when Titan goes to bed ;
>   Or a shady bush or tree,—
>   Sho could more infuse in me
>   Than all Nature's beauties can
>   In some other wiser man."

Surely this is the voice of Wordsworth in Tudor phraseology. Still more startling is this passage from Marvell, out of the midst of the Commonwealth days : so remarkable is its Nature Mysticism and its Wordsworthian feeling and insight, that it must be given without curtailment. It occurs in the poem on the "Garden."

> " Meanwhile the mind, from pleasure less,
>   Withdraws into its happiness ;
>   The mind, that ocean where each kind
>   Does straight its own resemblance find ;
>   Yet it creates, transcending these,
>   Far other worlds, and other seas,
>   Annihilating all that's made
>   To a green thought in a green shade,
>   Here at the fountain's sliding foot,
>   Or at some fruit-tree's mossy root,
>   Casting the body's vest aside,
>   My soul into the boughs does glide :
>   There, like a bird, it sits and sings,
>   Then whets and combs its silver wings,
>   And, till prepared for longer flight,
>   Waves in its plumes the various light."

Nature Mysticism

Every line of this extract is worthy of close study—not only for its intrinsic beauty, but for its evidence of the working of the immanent ideas, and the vivid sense of kinship with tree life. The two lines

> " Annihilating all that's made
>   To a green thought in a green shade,"

are justly famous. But more significant are the three less known ones :

> " Casting the body's vest aside
>   My soul into the boughs does glide :
>   There like a bird it sits and sings."

Did Wordsworth, or Tennyson, or Shelley, ever give token of a more vivid sense of kinship with the life of the tree ? Is it not palpable that the same essential form of intuitive experience is struggling in each and all of these poets to find some fitting expression ? For Marvell, as for Wordsworth,

> " The soft eye-music of slow-waving boughs "

seemed to fluctuate with an interior life and to call for joyous sympathy.

Or, finally, study these passages from Walt Whitman, the sturdy Westerner ; his feeling for the mystic impulses from tree life is exceptional, if not in its intensity, at any rate in his determination to give it utterance. If trees do not talk, he says, they certainly manage it " as well as most speaking, writing, poetry, sermons—or rather they do a great deal better. I should say indeed

that those old dryad reminiscences are quite as
true as any, and profounder than most, reminiscences we get." Farther on, speaking of evening
lights and shades on foliage grass, he says, " In
the revealings of such light, such exceptional hour,
such mood, one does not wonder at the old story
fables (indeed, why fables ?) of people falling into
love-sickness with trees, seiz'd ecstatic with the
mystic realism of the resistless silent strength in
them—strength which, after all, is perhaps the
last, completest, highest beauty." In another
place, he says, " I hold on boughs or slender trees
caressingly there in the sun and shade, wrestle
with their inmost stalwartness—and *know* the
virtue thereof passes from them into me. (Or
maybe we interchange—maybe the trees are more
aware of it all than I ever thought.)" And once
again, speaking of a yellow poplar tree, " How
strong, vital, enduring ! How dumbly eloquent !
What suggestions of imperturbability and *being*,
as against the human trait of *seeming*. Then the
qualities, almost emotional, palpably artistic,
heroic, of a tree ; so innocent and harmless, yet
so savage. It *is*, yet says nothing. How it rebukes
by its tough and equable serenity all weathers."
All this is unconventional ! So much the better !
The identity of underlying sentiment comes out
the more clearly. Trees are not only alive (and
yet how much that fact alone contains !) but
they have a character, an individuality of their
own ; they can speak directly to the heart

Nature Mysticism

and soul of man, and man can sympathise with them.

As for the animal world in the widest sense, it is plain that its study, from the mystical point of view, forms a department to itself. Granted that the transition from the mineral to the organism is gradual, and that from the vegetable to the animal still more gradual, the broad fact remains that, when we reach the higher forms of the realm of living matter, we definitely recognise many of the characteristics which are found in the human soul—will, emotion, impulse, even intellectual activities. Not only primitive man, but those also who are often far advanced in mental development, attribute souls to animals, and find it difficult to believe otherwise—as witness the totemistic systems followed by theories of metempsychosis. And Darwinism, far from destroying these old ideas, has simply furnished a scientific basis for a new totemism.

As was remarked at the outset, this subject of what we may call Animal Mysticism, lies outside our present province. Nevertheless, a word or two showing how the physical, the vegetable, and the animal are linked together in living mystical union may fittingly bring this chapter to a close. Many of our deepest and most original thinkers are feeling their way to this larger Mysticism. Here are two examples taken almost at random. Anatole France, in one of the many charming episodes which render his story of the old savant, Sylvestre

Seasons, Vegetation, Animals

Bonnard, at once so touching and so philosophic, takes his old hero under the shade of some young oaks to meditate on the nature of the soul and the destiny of man. The narrative proceeds thus: "Une abeille, dont le corsage brun brillait au soleil comme une armure de vieil or, vint se poser sur une fleur de mauve d'une sombre richesse et bien ouverte sur sa tige touffue. Ce n'était certainement pas la première fois que je voyais un spectacle si commun, mais c'était la première que je le voyais avec une curiosité si affectueuse et si intelligente. Je reconnus qu'il y avait entre l'insecte et la fleur toutes sortes de sympathies et mille rapports ingénieux que je n'avais pas soupçonnés jusque là. L'insecte, rassasié de nectar, s'élança en ligne hardie. Je me relevai du mieux que je pus, et me rajustai sur mes jambes—Adieu, dis-je à la fleur et à l'abeille. Adieu. Puissé-je vivre encore le temps de deviner le secret de vos harmonies. , . . Combien le vieux mythe d'Antée est plein de sens ! J'ai touché la terre et je suis un nouvel homme, et voici qu'à soixante-dix ans de nouvelles curiosités naissent dans mon âme comme on voit des rejetons s'élancer du tronc creux d'un vieux saule."

"May I live long enough to solve the secret of your harmonies !" There is the spirit of the true nature-mystic ! But how will it be solved ? By intuition first—if ever the intellect does seize the secret, it will be on the basis of intuition. It is with this conviction in his mind that Maeterlinck

255

Nature Mysticism

meditates on the same theme as that which arrested Anatole France. "Who shall tell us, oh, little people (the bees), that are so profoundly in earnest, that have fed on the warmth and the light and on nature's purest, the soul of the flowers—wherein matter for once seems to smile and put forth its most wistful effort towards beauty and happiness—who shall tell us what problems you have resolved, but we not yet; what certitudes you have acquired, that we have still to conquer ? And if you have truly resolved these problems, acquired these certitudes, by the aid of some blind and primitive impulse and not through the intellect, then to what enigma, more insoluble still, are you not urging us on ? "

Such is the leaven that is working in much of the foremost thinking of our time. The reign of materialism is passing—that of mysticism waxing in imperative insistence and extent of sway. And the heart of the nature-mystic rejoices to know that his master-principle of kinship universal is coming to its own. Anatole France and Macterlinck are striving to seize on the harmonies between the physical, the vegetable, and the animal spheres—the air and sunshine, the flowers, and the bees ; add the moral and spiritual harmonies, and Mysticism stands complete—it strives to read the secret of existence as a whole, of the " *élan vital* " in this or any other world.

CHAPTER XXXIV

PRAGMATIC

THE programme laid down in the introductory chapter has been fulfilled. There has been no attempt to make any single section, much less the study as a whole, a complete or exhaustive exposition of its subject matter. The purpose throughout has been to bring to light the fundamental principles of Nature Mysticism, to consider the validity of the main criticisms to which they are subjected, and to illustrate some of their most typical applications. A formal summary of the conclusions reached would be tedious and unnecessary. But it may be well to show that even when brought to the tests imposed by the reigning Pragmatism, the nature-mystic can justify his existence and can proselytise with a good conscience.

" Back to the country "—a cry often heard, though generally with a significance almost wholly economic, or at any rate utilitarian. It gives expression to the growing conviction that the life of great cities is too artificial and specialised to permit of a healthy all-round development of their populations. From the eugenic point of view, physique is lowered. From the economic point of view, large areas are deprived of their healthy independence by the disturbance of the balance of production as between town and country. Each of these considerations is evidently of sufficient seriousness to arouse widespread apprehension.

But there is the nature-mystic's view of the situation which, when really attained, is seen to be of no less importance, though it is too often left in comparative obscurity. It is easily approached from the purely æsthetic side. The city may develop a quick and precocious intelligence, but it is at the cost of eliminating a rich range of experiences which should be the heritage of all normal human beings. In the city, the mind tends to be immersed in a restricted and specialised round of duties and pleasures, and loses " natural " tone. While, on the one hand, there is over-stimulation of certain modes of sensation, others are largely or wholly atrophied. The finest susceptibilities decay. The eye and ear, the most delicate avenues of the soul, are deprived of their native stimulants. In short, city conditions unduly inhibit the natural development of many elements of the higher self.

The evils thus briefly touched upon are undoubtedly forcing themselves more and more into notice, and are evoking much philanthropic thought and activity. They are more especially bewailed by many who, themselves lovers of art and lovers of nature, keenly appreciate the loss sustained, and the danger incurred. Ruskin's teachings have

Pragmatic

affected the views and lives of thousands who have never read his books. Those who have penetrated most deeply into the play of æsthetic cause and effect, well know that the very existence of truly great and creative art is at stake. Science, literature, politics, and a thousand specialised distractions tend to "saturate our limited attention," and to absorb our energies, to the detriment of our feeling for nature and of our enjoyment of her beauties. And yet it is only by keeping in living touch with nature that fine art can renew its inspiration or scale the heights.

There is, of course, the counter peril of an unhealthy æstheticism, marked by an assumption of susceptibility which is insufferable. Feeling, ostensibly expended upon external beauty, can become an odious form of self-admiration; and priggishness is the least of the diseases that will ensue. For with the loss of spontaneity and freshness in the feeling there goes mortification of the feeling itself. Still, this danger is not general, and is therefore less noteworthy. It may safely be left to the healing remedies instinctively applied by common sense.

The nature-mystic, however, does not linger long on the merely æsthetic plane. He goes deeper down to the heart of things, and holds that to lose touch with nature is to lose touch with Reality as manifested in nature. It is sad, he declares, to miss the pure enjoyment of forms and colours, of sounds and scents; it is sadder to miss the experience of communing with the spirit embodied in these external phenomena. For it is not mere lack of education of the senses that must then be lamented (though that is lack enough!) but the stunting of the soul-life that ensues on divorce from nature, and from the great store of primal and fundamental ideas which are immanent therein. The loss may thus become, not simply sad, but tragic.

And the weightiness of these considerations is not diminished when we relate them to the special needs of the day. Our time is one of deep unrest— showing itself in religion and ethics, in literature and art, in politics and economics. Unrest manifests itself in what we have learnt to call " the social question." How shall civilisation regain and increase its healthy restfulness? Unless a cure be found, there will be disaster ahead. Democracy has brought with it great hopes; it also stirs unwonted fears. The people at large must be lifted on to a higher plane of living; they must win for themselves wider horizons; they must kindle their imaginations, and allow play to their non-egoistic and nobler emotions. How better secure these ends than by bringing " the masses " into touch with the elemental forces and phenomena of nature? " Democracy " (says Walt Whitman) " most of all affiliates with the open air, is sunny and hardy and sane only with Nature—just as much as Art is. Something is required to temper both—to check them, restrain them from excess, morbidity. . . . I conceive of no flourishing and heroic elements of

Pragmatic

Democracy . . . without the Nature element forming a main part—to be its health-element and
beauty-element—to really underlie the whole
politics, sanity, religion, and art of the New
World." Yes, converse with Nature—even the
simplest form of converse—has a steadying effect,
and brings that kind of quiet happiness which has
for its companions good-will and delicate sympathy. To sever oneself from such converse is to
induce selfishness, boorishness (veneered or un-
veneered), and inhumanity. The influence of
nature means development; the lack of that
influence means revolution.

Hence Wordsworth's invitation has its social,
as well as its individual bearings :

> " Up ! up ! my Friend, and quit your books,
> Or surely you'll grow double !
>
> .   .   .   .   .   .
>
> One impulse from a vernal wood
> May teach you more of man,
> Of moral evil and of good,
> Than all the sages can.
>
> Sweet is the lore which Nature brings ;
> Our meddling intellect
> Mis-shapes the beauteous forms of things
> We murder to dissect.
>
> Enough of Science and of Art ;
> Close up those barren leaves ;
> Come forth and bring with you a heart
> That watches and receives."

261

Nature Mysticism

So Emerson, of the man who can yield himself to nature's influences. "And this is the reward: that the ideal shall be real to thee, and the impressions of the actual world shall fall like summer rain, copious but not troublesome, to thy invulnerable essence." So, once again, Matthew Arnold in his striking sonnet, "Quiet Work":

"One lesson, Nature, let me learn of thee,
One lesson which in every wind is blown,
One lesson of two duties kept at one
Though the loud world proclaim their enmity—
Of toil unsevered from tranquillity,
Of labour that in lasting fruit outgrows
Far noisier schemes, accomplished in repose,
Too great for haste, too high for rivalry.
Yes, while on earth a thousand discords ring,
Man's senseless uproar mingling with his toil,
Still do thy quiet ministers move on,
Their glorious tasks in silence perfecting:
Still working, blaming still our vain turmoil,
Labourers that shall not fail when man is gone."

It is in nature, then, and in her subtle but potent workings on the human soul that we shall find at least one antidote for the undue and portentous tension of our day. To say this is not to depreciate science, but to put it in its rightful setting. Nor is it to depreciate culture, but to bring it into due perspective, and to vitalise it. Nor is it to depreciate art, but to endow it with glow, with variety, with loyalty to truth.

According to Pope, the proper study of mankind is man. How shallow, how harmful such a dictum !

Pragmatic

Contrast Kant's deeper insight. "Two things fill me with awe—the starry heaven without, and the moral law within." That famous apophthegm leads us nearer to the saving truth. For it contemplates man, not in his isolation, but as placed in a marvellous physical environment : to understand one you must understand the other also. Add the thought expressed in the fundamental principle of Nature Mysticism—the thought that nature is spiritually akin to ourselves—and we see that the proper study of mankind is human nature as a part of a living whole.

But the nature-mystic is not content to " study." He desires to hold communion with the spirit and the life which he feels and knows to be manifested in external nature. For him there is no such thing as " brute " matter, nor even such a thing as " mere " beauty. He hears deep calling unto deep—the life within to the life without—and he responds.